THE

Church and Slavery.

BY

ALBERT BARNES.

PHILADELPHIA:
PARRY & McMILLAN,
SUCCESSORS TO A. HART, LATE CAREY & HART.
1857.

STEREOTYPED BY L. JOHNSON AND CO.
PHILADELPHIA.

PRINTED BY T. K. AND P. G. COLLINS.

THE

Church and Slavery.

INTRODUCTION.

THERE are times when it is important that every man, however humble may be his name, should express his views on great moral, political, and religious subjects. Public sentiment is made up of a great number of individual opinions, as earth and ocean are made up of a great number of individual particles of matter. The opinion of each individual contributes to form the public sentiment, as the labour of the animalcule in the ocean contributes to form the coral reefs that rise above the waves.

Public sentiment controls our land; public sentiment will ultimately control the world. All that error, tyranny, and oppression demand is a strong public sentiment in their favor; all that is necessary to counteract their influence is that public sentiment should be right.

The present is eminently a time when the views of every man on the subject of slavery should be uttered in unambiguous tones. There has never been but one thing that has perilled the existence of the American Union, and that one thing is slavery. There has never been a time when the Union was really in danger until now. There has never been a time when the system of slavery has been so bold, exacting, arrogant, and dangerous to liberty, as at present. There has never been a time when so much importance, therefore, could be attached to the views of individual men; when so much could be done in favor of the rights of man by a plain utterance of sentiment; when so much guilt would be incurred by silence. It cannot be right that any one who holds the system to be evil in its origin, evil in its bearing on the morals of men, evil in its relations to religion, evil in its influence on the master and the slave—on the body and the soul—on the North and the South, evil in its relations to time and in its relations to eternity, should so act that it shall be possible to misunderstand his opinions in relation to it,—so act that his conduct could be appealed to as implying an apology for the system. The circle in which he moves may be a limited circle; his views may influence but few of the living, and may cease to be regarded altogether when he is dead; but for the utterance of those views, and for the position which he takes on this as on other subjects, he must soon give an account at a tribunal where silence on great moral subjects, as well as an open defence of what is wrong, will be regarded and treated as guilt. No man, therefore, should allow himself on these great questions to be in such a position that, by any fair construction of his life and opinions, his influence, however humble it may be, should be made to sustain error and wrong, or be of such a nature that his name can be referred to as furnishing a support for cruelty and oppression.

As it is true that the only thing that ever has threatened to destroy this Union, or that now threatens to destroy it, is slavery, so it is true that the only thing that alienates one portion of the land from the other is slavery. In language, in customs, in laws, in religion, we are, and always have been, otherwise, a united people. We have a common origin. We all look to the same "fatherland," and we all claim that the glory of that land, in literature, in science, and in the arts, is a part of our common inheritance. We look back to the times of the Revolution; and, whatever wisdom there was in council, or whatever valour there was in battle, or whatever there was that was self-sacrificing in the cause of liberty, is a part of the common inheritance of this generation. Our railroads spread a network over all the States, making them one. Simultaneously through all the States of the Union the telegraph bears to millions of minds at once what is of common interest to all. Some of our great rivers roll along through vast States, Northern and Southern; and by our location, and by all the varieties of climate and soil constituting mutual dependence, we are designed by nature to be one people. On the question of slavery only are we divided. This question meets us everywhere, generates all the bad feeling there is between the North and the South, subjects us to all the reproach that we encounter from abroad; and it is the source of all that tends to produce civil strife, to cause alienation and discord in the churches, or to embroil us with the nations of the earth.

It cannot but be an inquiry of great importance how far *the church* is connected with this state of things, and how far, if at all, it is responsible for it. In a country so extensively under the influence of religion as ours; where religion undeniably so much controls public sentiment; where so large a portion of the community is connected with the church; and where the Christian ministry exerts so wide an influence on the public mind, it cannot be an unimportant question what the church *is* doing, and what it *ought* to do, in reference to an evil so vast, and so perilous to all our institutions.

I write over my own name. It is not because I suppose that my name will have any special claim in influencing the public mind; and not because I suppose it to be important that I should "define my position," as if the public had any particular interest in my position; and not because I suppose that the public will concern itself long to learn how any one individual thinks or feels on any subject that he may deem of special importance; but because I think it fair and manly that a man should be willing to attach his name to any sentiments which he holds, and which he chooses, for any reason, to submit to the consideration of mankind. I have no wish also to deny that I desire that my name should be found associated with any well-directed effort to remove slavery from the earth. I believe that the religion which I profess is opposed in its whole spirit and tendency to slavery; that its fair and legitimate application would remove the last remnant of it from the world; and that in every effort which I may make to show to my fellow-men the evils of the system, or to promote universal emancipation, I am performing the appropriate duty of a Christian man, and of a minister of the gospel of Christ.

CHAPTER I.

THE GENERAL RELATION OF THE CHURCH TO SLAVERY.

In forming a correct view of the subject, it is important, first of all, to ascertain what is the actual relation of the church to slavery, or how the church becomes interested in the questions that pertain to it, and what responsibility it sustains in regard to it; then to inquire what is the actual position of the church in regard to it; and then what is the duty of the church, in the present state of things in our country, in regard to it. I write with special reference to my own denomination; but at the same time I shall write in such a manner as to show what is the general relation which the various denominations of Christians in this land sustain to the system. There is an essential brotherhood in the family of Christian churches in regard to what is good. Alas! it is to be feared that there is, to a great extent, a fearful brotherhood in those churches in sustaining enormous evils.

The following facts, then, will be admitted to be undeniable; and they will show how the church becomes interested in the questions relating to slavery.

1. Not a few church-members are slave-holders. Compared, indeed, with *all* the members of the church in the land, or compared with those who are slave-holders who are not members of the church,

the number is few; but in the aggregate the number of members of the church, in all the religious denominations, who hold their fellow-men in bondage, is not small. I am not aware that the exact number of slave-holders in any denomination has been ascertained, nor do I know of any *data* by which a probable approximation to the number could be made; but the fact that there are such members of the church, and that the number in the aggregate is not small, it would be as impossible to deny as it is painful to admit it. It is to be conceded, also, that a portion of these are ministers of the gospel and others who bear important offices, and who sustain important stations in the churches. It is to be admitted, also, that of these church-members, embracing also, it is to be feared, some who are ministers of the gospel, there are those who are slave-holders in the most rigid and offensive sense,— who hold slaves not merely by inheritance, or by a legal relation for the good of the slave; who hold them not because they are aged and need a protector; who hold them not *in transitu* and for the purpose of emancipating them; who hold them not as *preparing* them for freedom, and with properly-executed instruments which would secure their freedom should they themselves die; who hold them under none of the forms of mere guardianship and for the purpose of humanity, but *as slaves*, as property, as chattels, as liable to be disposed of like the other portions of their estate when they die. There are those also in the churches who purchase and sell slaves as they do any other property; who buy them that they may avail themselves of their unrequited labour; and who sell them as they do any other property, for the sake of gain. It is to be admitted, also, that there are those who thus hold slaves under laws which forbid their being taught to read, and who comply with those laws; under laws which restrain their religious liberty, and who comply with those laws; under laws which prevent all proper formation of the marriage-relation, and all proper organization of the family-relation, and who comply with those laws; and under laws which, when a man dies, make his slaves liable to be sold for the payment of his debts,—like any other part of his property. It is to be admitted, also, that there are those connected with the Christian churches who hold their slaves under laws which furnish no security for maintaining the relation between man and wife, and parents and children, among their slaves, and who lift up no voice of remonstrance against the iniquity of those laws, and make no effort to secure their own slaves from the tremendous evils inflicted on human beings by their operation. If this is a fact, one source of the interest which the church has in the subject of slavery will be at once apparent; if this is a fact, no one can question the propriety of an appeal to the church on the subject.

2. Not a few ministers of the gospel, and members of the churches, either apologize for slavery, or openly defend it, even as it exists in the United States. It is not affirmed here that the proportion of those who thus apologize for slavery, or who defend it, as compared with those who entertain other views, is large, or that a majority of the ministers of religion or members of the churches in the land are impli-

cated in the guilt of defending the system; and it cannot be denied that gross injustice is often done to the ministers of the gospel in this country, and to members of the churches, by charging on all that which belongs only to a part, and much the smallest part, of the entire body. But still the following facts are undeniable:—

(*a*) There are those, as has been already remarked, who are themselves slave-holders, and, so far as appears, slave-holders in the proper sense of the term: holding their fellow-men in bondage, not as guardians, not as sustaining merely the legal relation with a view to their freedom, not as educating them for freedom, and not making provision for their emancipation, but *as slaves*,—as property,—with a view to worldly gain from the relation, and without remonstrance against the oppressive laws which withhold from them the word of God, and which regard them as liable to be treated like any other property in case of the death of the master.

(*b*) There are those who defend the system as one authorized by the Bible, and as having for its sanction the authority of God; who refer to it as a "patriarchal" institution, sustained by the example of the holy men of early times, and as not, as they allege, discountenanced by the teaching of the Saviour and his apostles. This number is not, indeed, large; but no one can doubt that there are those in the church who occupy this position, and whose aid is relied on by those who wish to make the system perpetual in the land.

(*c*) There are those who, while they are not themselves slave-holders, and are not open advocates of the system, and who would consider that great injustice was done them if they were represented as pro-slavery men, yet regard the system as substantially on the same foundation as the other relations in life;—not wrong in itself, wrong only in its abuses. Thus, the relation of "master and servant" is compared with the relation of husband and wife, and parent and child, and landlord and tenant, and guardian and ward, and master and apprentice,—relations growing out of the constitution of things, or springing up in the necessities of society, and, as such, relations which may be expected always to exist in the world. By this class of ministers and church members, it is sometimes affirmed that the relation is founded on the judgment of God on a doomed race,—the descendants of Ham; sometimes that it is founded on the inferiority of the African race; sometimes that it is justified by the difference of complexion, sometimes by the alleged fact that, incapable of guiding themselves, they need the guardianship and protection of a superior race, and sometimes by the alleged fact that it is only in this way that the African can be raised to a participation in the blessings of civilization and Christianity. Whatever may be the foundation of the representation, the essential idea is that the relation is one that is *lawful*, or that it is on the same basis as the lawful relations of human society. For the *abuses* of the system they would hold men responsible, as they would in the relation of parents and children, and master and apprentice, but not for the relation itself any more in the one case than in the other. According to this view, the fact of being a slave-holder furnishes no more presumption against a man's Christian character than the fact of being a husband and father, or than the fact of being at the head of a large mercantile or manufacturing establishment: for the abuse of power in either case, and precisely for the same reasons, he would be justly responsible, and would incur blame; but not for the mere *relation* in the one case more than in the other.

(*d*) There are those in the ministry, and those who are private members of the churches, who, whatever may be their real sentiments, are, from their position, their silence, or their avowed conservatism, classed in public estimation with the apologists for slavery, and whose aid can never be relied on in any efforts for the emancipation of those who are in bondage. They have attached an importance to the modern idea of *conservatism* which cannot be justified by any reference to the teachings of the Bible, or the life and doctrines of the Saviour,—an idea which makes it possible to plead their example in favour of that which is *wrong*, as well as of that which is *right.* They regard that which is fixed and settled as so important that it is better that a wrong should be endured, rather than to peril the safety of existing institutions by any change whatever. They have affixed to the Union of the States such a value that it is fairly inferred from their opinion that it is better that any evil should be endured—that any number of millions of human beings should be held in hopeless bondage—than that the existence of the Union should be perilled. They have affixed an odious idea to the word *abolitionist*, and, so far as their influence goes, led the public to do it also;

surrounding it with all that is disorganizing and radical, with all that is repulsive in fanaticism and dangerous in politics, with all that is hateful in intermeddling in the concerns of others, and with all that arouses the soul in the idea of *treason.* With this name, also, this class of ministers of the gospel, and these members of the churches, endeavour to associate the idea of infidelity; and, because some who have assumed the name have rejected the Bible and denounced the Christian church and the Christian ministry as upholders of this enormous evil, their influence in fact goes to convey the inference that abolitionism and infidelity are really if not quite identical, and that to attempt to emancipate the slave would be an attempt to spread the evils of skepticism through the land.

(*e*) There are editors of religious papers, and authors of books connected with the Christian church, whose opinions are of great value to slaveholders in defending the system of slavery. If there is no formal and avowed *defence* of slavery, and even if there is an occasional formal statement that they are personally opposed to the system, yet their influence is such as to make it possible and convenient to refer to them in support of the system. Their words of condemnation are so cold, so formal, so few and so far between, that with the advocates of the system they pass for mere form. They speak of the relation of master and slave as they do of any other relation; they inculcate the duties of the master and the duties of the slave as they do the duties of the parent and the duties of the child, with the underlying idea that the relations are equally lawful and designed to be equally permanent. They enjoin on the slave submission to his condition, as they do on the poor man contentment in his poverty, as if both were in the same sense among the fixed though mysterious arrangements of Providence. They adduce arguments from the Bible in regard to the relation which are gratifying in an eminent degree to the slave-holder, and they adopt such expositions of the Bible as are exactly what he desires in order to sustain him in his position and to sanction his holding his fellow-men in bondage. They employ words in regard to the system so smooth that, if they do not actually furnish a formal defence of the evil, yet will not disturb the sleep of the slave-holder, but are rather fitted to give ease to his conscience and to impart to him quiet slumbers and pleasant dreams. Meantime they make use of just such words and just such arguments in regard to abolitionism as to be grateful in the highest degree to slave-holders themselves. No one can doubt that not a few of the conductors of the religious press in this country are constantly thus expressing views which are eminently gratifying to slave-holders as such, and which are among the means by which they sustain themselves in their position and by which they justify themselves in holding their fellow-men in bondage.

3. Large portions of the church are in the midst of slavery. The institutions which surround the church are those which are connected with slavery and which take a peculiar cast and complexion from slavery. In many respects those institutions

are different from similar institutions where freedom prevails. The customs of society are different. The intercourse in social life is different. The modes of speech are different. The views entertained of labour are different. The views of rank and position in society are different. They who are in the condition of domestics or servants are regarded and treated in a different manner. A different kind of deference towards their superiors is expected, and a different mode of treating them and of speaking to them is expected. Children at the North and the South grow up with different modes of speech and behaviour, and they enter on life with different views of the essential organization of society. Slavery touches on society at a thousand different points; and it is impossible that there should be *any* institution in a region where slavery prevails which will not be more or less affected by it.

Besides, though the churches located in the midst of slavery may be wholly free from any direct participation in it, it is still true that the church is designed to influence all surrounding institutions. This is a part of its mission in the world,—a part of the reason why it is established and perpetuated on the earth. The church often springs up in the midst of a mass of moral corruption for the very purpose of modifying by its influence existing institutions, and changing the whole aspect of society. Pure in itself, it sheds a benign influence on all around, and its contact with prevailing institutions rebukes what is wrong and suggests and sanctions what is right. By a healthful contact it diffuses moral purity through a community. A church, therefore, located in the midst of slavery, though all its members may be wholly unconnected with slavery, yet owes an important duty to society and to God in reference to the system; and its mission will not be accomplished by securing merely the sanctification of its own members, or even by drawing within its fold multitudes of those who shall be saved. It is not merely by an orthodox faith, or by the pure lives of its own members, that it fulfils its work on the earth; it is not merely by its being the patron of schools and colleges, or by its influence in sending the gospel to heathen lands; it is not by the establishment of Sabbath-schools for the children of its own families, or by zeal in distributing Bibles and the publications of the Tract Society within its geographical limits, that its work is to be done. Its primary work as a church may have reference to an existing evil within its own geographical limits. The burden which is laid upon it may not be primarily the conversion of the heathen or the diffusion of Bibles and tracts abroad: the work which God requires it to do, and for which specifically it has been planted there, may be to diffuse a definite moral influence in respect to an existing evil institution. On all that is wrong in social life, in the modes of intercourse, in the habits of training the young, and in the prevailing sentiments in the community that have grown out of existing institutions, God may have planted the church there to exert a definite moral influence,—a work for himself. Whether it is to make a direct assault *on* such institutions may be another question; but there can be no difference of opinion as to the fact that a church thus situated *has* much to do with all existing institutions, and, therefore, with slavery; and that its influence in regard to that system is a part of the work which it is to accomplish in the world. In the nature of the case it cannot be otherwise than that it will, in very important respects, come in contact with slavery. The church will affect the institution of slavery, or the institution of slavery will affect the church. It will send out a healthful moral influence to secure its removal, or the system will send out a corrupt influence into the church itself, to mould the opinions of its members, to corrupt their piety, to make them apologists for oppression and wrong, and to secure its sanction in sustaining the system itself. Which will be the preponderating influence cannot be determined by mere conjecture. It would be a more sad and dark page in the history of the church than could be desired, if one should undertake to record the actual result. Whether, in our own country, it has moulded the system in the midst of which it is placed, or the system has moulded *it*, is an inquiry on which one who is desirous to show that the church has always exerted a good influence on the surrounding world would perhaps prefer to be silent.

4. The interest which the church has in the subject of slavery may be seen, in connection with the preceding remark, from the power which the church necessarily has on all great moral subjects. In reference to this the following things will commend themselves as worthy of attention:—

(*a*) The *number* of professing Christians in all parts of this land where slavery abounds, in the aggregate, is not small. Compared with the whole population, or with the whole number of slave-holders, or with the whole number of members in the great religious denominations in the land, we shall see, indeed, in another part of this Essay, that the number is *not* large; and yet it is probable that a community of slave-holders cannot be found where there is not a portion of the people who are either professors of religion, or who sustain an intimate relation to the church. No community of slave-holders in this land is made up of a heathen population; none of a population avowedly infidel. There is no such community in which the prevailing views in regard to slavery itself are derived from the speculations of heathen philosophers or moralists; none in which the authority of the Bible is professedly abjured; none in whieh the Sabbath and the sanctuary, the Sabbath-school and the prayer-meeting, are wholly unknown. The mass of slave-holders themselves, though not professing Christians, are not avowed infidels; nor is it known that infidelity prevails among them to a greater extent than it does in other portions of the community. Indeed, it would probably be found, from causes which need not now be inquired into, that avowed infidelity is less common at the South than at the North, and that there are fewer men, in the States where slavery prevails, who would be willing to take the position of open rejection of the Bible, than there are amidst the freer institutions of the North.

(*b*) The church *has* influence in all such places. The men who compose it are not altogether those of the humbler ranks, or those who have little or nothing at stake in society. A respectable portion of the members of the church, in places where slavery prevails as well as elsewhere, is composed of men of wealth, of education, and of elevated standing in the community. Not a few occupy public positions; not a few are members of the learned professions; and no one can doubt that, *as* members of the church, they do much to control the public mind on the subject of morals.

(*c*) Again: In our country there is no class of men who exert more influence than ministers of the gospel; and there is, perhaps, no portion of the land where ministers of the gospel in fact exert more influence than they do in slave-holding communities. Probably there is no part of the land where they mingle so freely in social life. There is no portion of the land where they are admitted more readily to the intimacies of families, or where their presence is regarded as more desirable in society. It should be added, also, that there is no part of the land where more *time* is actually spent by ministers of the gospel in social life, or in free, pleasant, and familiar intercourse with the people. From the nature of the prevalent habits in the free States, where so few men have leisure for social intercourse, it is undoubtedly a fact that ministers of the gospel are much more a distinct portion of the community — under a much stronger inducement to withdraw from social life — than in slave-holding communities; and, if there is any portion of the land where ministers of the gospel enjoy peculiar facilities for influencing the public mind, directly and indirectly, it would seem to be in the slave-holding States. And, as no one could estimate the power which ministers of the gospel *might* have, in such communities, in removing this evil, so no one can estimate the actual influence which they *do* exert in sustaining and perpetuating it. If it should be found to be true that they are silent on this subject while they freely denounce all other forms of sin,—if it should be true that they apologize for it as they would not dare or wish to do for intemperance, Sabbath-breaking, licentiousness, gambling or, lotteries,—if it should be true that they refer to this relation as they do to the relations of husband and wife, parent and child, master and apprentice, landlord and tenant,—if it should be true that they make a frequent reference, and one quite satisfactory to slave-holders, to the institution of slavery as 'patriarchal,' implying that the slavery now existing is of the same nature as that which existed in patriarchal times, or implying that the sanction of a patriarch gave authority to slavery any more than it did to polygamy or fraud,—if it should be true that they indulge in great freedom of language, and language everyway gratifying to slave-holders, in regard to abolitionists, and that they usually represent the fact of being an abolitionist as being synonymous with being an infidel, a fanatic, a disorganizer, or an enemy of the Union,—then it is clear that no one can estimate the actual influence of the ministers of the gospel in sustaining slavery, and no one can fail to see that the church *has* an important interest in the great questions respecting slavery and freedom.

(*d*) Again, to recur a moment to a point already referred to:—There is a large number of editors of papers and authors of books who are connected with the church, and whose influence *must* be great in regard to questions like those which pertain to slavery. Not a few of those editors and authors are educated ministers of the gospel; and the community is accustomed to look up to them, as ministers and as conductors of the press, for the formation of its opinions on moral subjects. No class of men, perhaps, exert a wider influence than the conductors of the press; and on no subject is that influence more likely to be referred to as forming the public mind than on the subject of slavery. It is easy, therefore, to see that the church in this respect *may* have a very intimate connection with slavery. If the conductors of the press—and especially of the religious press—shall be found to speak of slavery as a scriptural, a permanent, or a 'patriarchal' institution,—if they more frequently refer to the comparatively dark and barbarous times when the patriarchs lived than to the teachings of the Saviour,—if they make constant reference to it as an institution that is on the same basis as the relations of master and apprentice, husband and wife, parent and child,—if their sympathy is *always* with the master and *never* with the slave, *always* with those portions of the country where slavery prevails and *never* with any others,—if, instead of seeing *no* North, *no* South, they see *only* the South, —if they are loud in their denunciations of abolitionists, and liberal in the use of the terms 'fanatics' and 'disorganizers,' as applied to them,—

and especially if they have had the misfortune to be bred at the North, and have then lived so long at the South, and been so long under Southern influence, that they can refer to their own observation as to the real facts about slavery as placing them on higher ground, in judging of the teachings of the Bible and the principles of religion, liberty, and morals, than men can possibly occupy who have never witnessed the happy workings of the system, —then it is clear that the friends of slavery must regard the influence of such men as of inestimable value in their cause, and that nothing could be better adapted to soothe the conscience of the slaveholder, and to satisfy him that in sustaining this relation he is "doing God service."

CHAPTER II.

THE ACTUAL INFLUENCE OF THE CHURCH ON THE SUBJECT OF SLAVERY.

If now it be asked, What is the actual influence of the church at large in regard to slavery? the following facts cannot but be regarded as undeniable:—

1. It is probable that slavery could not be sustained in this land if it were not for the countenance, direct and indirect, of the churches. That is, if all the churches should assume in regard to it the position which the society of Friends has done, and which some of the Scotch and German churches have done, and simply *detach* themselves from it, it is probable that there is not power enough *out* of the church to sustain the system. It is not true, indeed, that the church is in any proper sense the 'bulwark of slavery;' for, taking the church at large since the time when it first found slavery established in the Roman empire, no other cause has operated so effectually in restraining and removing it as the influence of the church; and, taking the church at large in our own country, it is not true that it sustains or defends the system. The great opponents of the system, at all times, have been, for the most part, members of the Christian church and professed followers of the Sa-

viour. What did Herbert and Chubb and Bolingbroke do in emancipating the slave? What did *not* Clarkson and Wilberforce do? What has heathenism ever done in emancipating the slave? What has Mohammedanism? What have heroes and philosophers, as such, done? It was by the influence of Christianity that slavery was abolished in the Roman empire. It was by the same influence that emancipation occurred in the British empire. And it is still true that the most decided influence adverse to slavery in this land has come from the bosom of the Christian church. But it is also true that, while the church is not the bulwark of slavery, there is not power enough out of the church to sustain it if the church were wholly detached from it and arrayed against it. Let the facts just stated be borne in mind, respecting the number of members of the church who are slave-holders, the number of ministers of the gospel in the same position, the silence of many of the ministers and churches in regard to the evil, the views entertained by many of the ministers of the gospel adapted to soothe the consciences of slave-holders, the influence of the religious press, and the fact that the institution is placed, by such ministers and editors and authors, on the same basis as the relation of husband and wife, and master and apprentice, as a permanent and lawful relation, and as implying no more blame or guilt than those relations; and let it be supposed that all this was reversed, and that all this influence was arrayed against the system, and that the whole Christian population of the land was in all respects not only detached from it, but arrayed against it:

would there be influence enough *out* of the church to perpetuate the system in the land?

2. It cannot be doubted that the views entertained and expressed by Christian ministers, and by others connected with the Christian church, in fact, do much to sustain slave-holders in their own views. It cannot but do much to relieve their consciences from trouble to know that the views which it is their interest to entertain are entertained by so large a portion of the Christian world. The conscience of the people of the world is little likely to be distressed or disturbed when the course which it wishes to pursue is sustained by the voice of the religious portion of the community. Whatever might be the views and feelings of slave-holders themselves if left to the admonitions of their own consciences, or if left to interpret the Bible for themselves, it is more than probable that they will welcome an interpretation of the Bible which coincides directly with their own interest, and that the fact that the Bible *is* thus interpreted will do much to allay any apprehensions which they may have of their own guilt. It is not probable that men in these circumstances, and with so much that is derived from *interest* to sustain them in their views, will regard that as deeply criminal which is sustained by so many occupying high positions in the religious world, or that they will apply themselves to any very close investigation in regard to the morality of a practice in which their own inclination, their own interest, and their own ease, all combine to induce them to believe that it is *not* immoral. It is, moreover, an undoubted fact that slaveholders *do* countenance those ministers who interpret the Bible in

accordance with what their own interest would suggest as a *desirable* interpretation; that they evince a much stronger affinity for those denominations of Christians who look with an indulgent eye on slavery than they do on those where it is made the subject of free discussion, and where a decided testimony is borne against it; and that they welcome to their families those religious papers which speak of it as a 'patriarchal' institution, and which place it on the same basis as the relation of master and apprentice, and husband and wife, rather than those which treat it as they do any other wrong relation and speak of the system as they do of any other evil. And it is undoubtedly true that those slave-holders who *desire* to find words of apology from others for slavery to sustain them in the practice,—who prefer relying on the judgment of others in matters where their own interest is concerned and where they desire that their consciences may not be troubled,—and who would be pleased to have in their families, and to have regularly circulated in a slave-holding community, religious papers in fact lending a sanction to slavery and placing it on the same level with lawful relations of life,—can find in the "religious press" of this country an ample gratification of their desires. There *are* papers professedly religious which express all that they could wish; and those papers come sustained and sanctioned by as respectable names of ministers of the gospel, and by as earnest and hearty commendations of ecclesiastical bodies, as could be desired. Indeed, if it be a fact that slave-holders *desire* from the church words of apology,—if they *wish* the countenance of ministers of religion to sustain them,—if they prefer *not* to investigate the Bible for themselves, from the apprehension that they would not find its spirit as favourable to slavery as they would desire, and would therefore prefer to rely on professed expositors of the Bible rather than on their own judgment,—and if they would wish for a class of newspapers to defend their institutions, and to brand all efforts to abolish slavery as fanaticism, and to suppress all discussion of the subject in ecclesiastical bodies,—it does not appear how they could adjust matters more to their own satisfaction than by the present arrangement. It is not easy to see what alterations they would themselves suggest in the course actually pursued by a considerable portion of the religious press in this country, or how, if all these were suspended, they could originate a plan that would better subserve their own wishes than they find now prepared to their hand. How many of the weekly newspapers that are now circulated in the region where slavery prevails, even those that are called 'religious,' are there that would be likely to disturb the conscience of a slave-holder? How many are there that would disabuse the mind of a slave-holder in regard to the character of the great mass who seek the abolition of slavery, and change the view that he is so much disposed to entertain,—that *all* abolitionists are fanatics? How many are there that would suggest to him a doubt whether the relation of master and slave is not as lawful as the relation of master and apprentice, of parent and child? How many religious tracts issued by the tract societies are there that would ever start the question in the mind of a slave-holder whether the relation *is* not as scriptural and lawful as the relation of master and apprentice, of guardian and ward?

3. In estimating the influence of the church on the subject of slavery, and the tendency of the representations made on the subject, it deserves to be considered how much is done by these representations to promote infidelity. There is a deep and growing conviction in the minds of the mass of mankind that slavery violates great laws of our nature; that it is contrary to the dictates of humanity; that it is essentially unjust, oppressive, and cruel; that it invades the rights of liberty with which the Author of our being has endowed all human beings; and that, in all the forms in which it has ever existed, it has been impossible to guard it from what its friends and advocates would call "*abuses* of the system." It is a violation of the first sentiments expressed in our Declaration of Independence, and on which our fathers founded the vindication of their own conduct in an appeal to arms; it is at war with all that a man claims for himself and for his own children; and it is opposed to all the struggles of mankind, in all ages, for freedom. The claims of humanity plead against it. The struggles for freedom everywhere in our world condemn it. The instinctive feeling in every man's own bosom in regard to himself is a condemnation of it. The noblest deeds of valour and of patriotism in our own land, and in all lands where men have struggled for freedom, are a condemnation of the system. All that is noble in man is opposed to it; all that is base, oppressive, and cruel, pleads for it. It is condemned by the in-

stinctive feelings of the human soul; it is condemned by the principles laid down in the books on morality that are placed in the hands of the young; it is condemned by the universal voice of history. There is nothing on which the sentiments of men *outside* of the church are coming to be more harmonious than in regard to the essential evil of slavery; there is nothing to which the course of things in the world, under the promptings of humanity, is more certainly tending, in all lands, than to the conviction that slavery is essentially evil and wrong, and that every human being, unless convicted of crime, has a right to freedom. There is nothing that finds a more hearty approbation from the world at large than an act of emancipation by a government; there is nothing that goes more permanently into the history of a nation than the changes in public affairs which result in such an act. There has been nothing that has more definitely marked the course of history, or constituted more marked epochs in history, than the successive steps which break the bonds of slavery and elevate men to the rank and dignity of freemen.

It is now impossible to convince the world that slavery is *right*, or is in accordance with the will of God. No decisions of councils or synods, and no teachings of a hierarchy, will change the onward course of opinion on this subject. No alleged authority of the Bible will satisfy men at large that the system is not always a violation of the laws that God has enstamped on the human soul. No apologies for it will take it out of the category of crime in the estimation of mankind at large, and place it in the category of virtues. The sentiment that it is wrong,—always wrong,—that it is a violation of the great laws of our being,—that it is contrary to the benevolent arrangements of the Maker of the race,—is becoming as fixed as the everlasting hills; and nothing can eradicate this sentiment from the hearts of mankind. This sentiment is becoming deeper and deeper in the convictions of the world every year; and, whatever may change, this is destined to remain unchangeably fixed. There is nothing more certain than that the world will *not* be brought to approve of slavery, and that the malediction of all good men will rest upon the system. No matter on what this sentiment impinges, it will be held; and nothing will be long held that is opposed to this deep conviction of the essential evil of the system. Men that are not otherwise disposed to be infidels *will* be infidels if, as the price of faith, they are required to abjure this conviction, and to hold that slavery is from God.

What, then, in this state of things, will be the effect of teaching that slavery is authorized by the Bible,—a professed revelation from God? That *in* that revelation slavery is contemplated as a permanent institution? That, according to the received interpretation, and the views of those who hold it to be a revelation from God, it is plainly implied that slavery is on the same basis as the relation of parent and child, guardian and ward, and as such is to be tolerated in the church, and to be among the things that are to be perpetuated and extended wherever the Bible controls human belief and conduct? That, according to the fair and received teachings of that book, it implies no more criminality to be a slave-holder than to be a father, a brother, or a neighbour? That the object of the Bible, so far as this is concerned, is to legislate *for* the system, and not to *remove* it; and that they who attempt to secure the emancipation of those held in bondage, and to impart to others the blessings of freedom, are 'radicals' and 'fanatics'? That to attempt to carry out practically the statement in the Declaration of Independence, that "*all* men are created equal," and "that they are endowed by their Creator with certain inalienable rights; that among these are life, LIBERTY, and the pursuit of happiness," is a violation of all the teachings of God's revealed will to mankind? That men who seek to transfuse into their own bosoms, in behalf of the African race, the sentiments which made Samuel Adams and John Hancock what they were, cherish feelings at war with revealed religion? And that men who seek to carry out practically what the world has been struggling for in the great battles of liberty, are 'fanatics' and 'disorganizers,'—are enemies of the plain teaching of the Bible, and rejecters of the word of God?

On many minds there *can* be but one result of such views. It will be, so far as these are regarded as the teachings of the Bible, to lead men to reject the Bible; to confirm skeptics in infidelity; and to furnish an argument to the rejecter of revelation which it will not be possible to answer. Such views impinge on great principles of human nature, and are at war with the teachings of God in the human soul, and with the lessons drawn from his dealings with the nations of the earth. All that is great and noble in man; all the instinctive aspirations for freedom in his own bosom; all his desires for liberty for himself and for his children; all the deep convictions in the soul in regard to human rights and the inestimable value of liberty, is at war with such teachings; and all the struggles for freedom in the world—all the lessons of history—go to confirm the impression that a book which contains such views of human bondage—which would place it among the lawful relations of life, and make provision for its being perpetual—CANNOT be from God. Men will say, and say in a form which cannot be met, 'If such are the teachings of the Bible, it is impossible that that book should be a revelation given to mankind from the true God. He has written, as if "graven with an iron pen and lead in the rock forever," other lessons than these on the souls of men; and both cannot be true. Nothing can be more certain than that man was formed by his Maker for freedom, and that all men have a right to be free. Nothing can be more true than the declaration in the immortal instrument which asserts our national independence, that "all men are created equal; that they are endowed by their Creator with certain inalienable rights; and that among these are life and LIBERTY." Nothing can be more certain than that God has implanted in the human soul a desire of liberty which is a fair expression of what he intends shall be the settled condition of things in the world. We want no book,' such men will go on to say, 'which proclaims other doctrines than these; we can embrace no book as a revelation from God which does not coincide with the great laws of our nature,—those laws which proclaim that all men have a right to be free. No book which departs in its teachings from those great laws CAN POSSIBLY BE FROM GOD.'

It is easy to see what would be the effect of similar teachings in any parallel case. Suppose it were alleged to be true that the Bible sanctioned polygamy, and that polygamy was regarded there as on the same basis as the original relation of marriage, or as any other lawful relation of life. Suppose that this was affirmed, by a large class of the best interpreters, to be the teaching of the Bible, and that it was so regarded by the church at large. And suppose that constant apologies were made for the institution of polygamy, and that it was maintained that men in this relation were responsible only for the *abuses* of the system,—for the quarrels, brawls, strifes, and jealousies that grow out of it. And suppose that the terms 'fanatics' and 'enemies of the Bible' were freely applied in the church to all who should call in question the lawfulness of polygamy, and seek to restore marriage to what seems to be an obvious law of nature,—the connection with one wife. What would be the effect of this doctrine in regard to the reception of the Bible as a revelation from God? In Pagan, Mohammedan, and Mormon regions it might not operate extensively in preventing the belief that it might be a divine revelation: but what would be the effect in a civilized land? Millions there are who could not, and would not, receive a book with such teachings as containing a revelation from God; and, whatever pretended external evidences such a book might have in its favour, they would say, 'We cannot receive it as containing the teachings of divine wisdom. God has organized society on a different basis; and a book containing such teachings cannot be from heaven.'

I believe that such inferences are legitimate, and that such reasoning cannot be answered. I believe that a pretended revelation, to be received in the world, must not contradict the great and eternal laws which God has written in the souls of men, and which have been incorporated into the very framework of social life. I do not believe that any book can make its way in the world as a revelation from God, or secure a permanent hold on the hearts of men as coming from him, which by its fair interpretation would teach that either polygamy or slavery is a lawful institution; that either is on the same moral basis as the relation of husband and wife, parent and child, master and apprentice, and that they are designed to be permanent relations in the world. But, at the same time, I do not believe that such are the fair teachings of the Bible; and I cannot, therefore, but regard all those who take this view of slavery as contributing, though undesignedly, to the defence and spread of infidelity. At all events, it is worth the serious consideration of all the real friends of religion, whether this effect is not actually produced in the land, and whether infidels are not thus furnished with a weapon against the Bible which it is not possible for those who entertain these views to answer.

It is not intrusion, then,—it is not becoming a "busybody in other men's matters,"—it is not impertinent and unlawful interference,—when the Christian church lifts up a voice of entreaty or of warning in regard to slavery. It is so placed that it cannot but be interested in the question; it is so related to the system that it must exert a vast if not a controlling influence in perpetuating it, or in removing it from our land and from the world.

CHAPTER III.

THE POSITION OF THE CHURCH AT LARGE ON THE SUBJECT OF SLAVERY.

Such being the case, it is important to inquire what is the actual position of the church in relation to slavery. The infidel has a right to ask this question; the Christian ought to be able to answer it.

The influence of the church is not, and has not been, what it might be; it is not what it should be. But, then, it should not be held responsible for what it cannot do; nor should its general influence be measured by the views of a small portion of its members. No body of men should be judged by the errors of a portion of its own body, or be charged as a whole with that which properly belongs only to a part. In respect to a portion of the church, we may admit that we have no words of apology to offer; while in the movements of other portions of it, and in the general effect of Christianity on the system for a period of one thousand eight hundred years, we may find much to justify the hope that its influence will be ultimately direct and decided in hastening the period when all mankind shall be free.

It would be wholly foreign to the design which I have in view, and would be a work which could not be accomplished in a volume of a few pages, to examine the general influence of the Christian church on the subject of slavery; and it would be equally apart from my design to examine in detail the position of other denominations of Christians than the one with which I am connected. My main object is to inquire into the actual position of my own denomination in regard to slavery, and the particular duty of that branch of the church of Christ. Yet, as connected with the general subject, and as tending to correct some prevalent misapprehensions in regard to the influence of the church on this great evil, and to meet some of the aspersions which are quite freely lavished upon the church by its enemies, it may be proper to make a few remarks on the general influence of the church on the subject.

The following facts, then, I suppose, do not admit of dispute:—

1. The *spirit* of the New Testament is against slavery, and the principles of the New Testament, if fairly applied, would abolish it. In the New Testament, no man is commanded to purchase and own a slave; no man is commended as adding any thing to the evidences of his Christian character, or as performing the appropriate duty of a Christian, for owning one. Nowhere in the New Testament is the institution referred to as a good one, or as a desirable one. It is commonly—indeed, it is almost universally—conceded that the proper application of the principles of the New Testament would abolish slavery everywhere, or that, in the state of things which will exist when the gospel shall be fairly applied to all the relations of life, slavery will not be found among those relations. This is admitted even

by most of those who apologize for slavery, and who, at other times, speak of it as on the same basis as the relation of husband and wife, or of master and apprentice. Moreover, it has not been often alleged by the enemies of Christianity that the New Testament sustains and sanctions slavery; that its spirit would be opposed to emancipation; or that the fair application of the gospel in the world would extend and perpetuate the system. There have been, and there are, keen-sighted and sagacious enemies of the Christian religion; there have been those who have had every disposition to show, if possible, that its influence in the world is evil; but it has not often occurred, so far as I know, that they have made it an objection to Christianity that its spirit was favourable to slavery, or that its fair application in the world would tend to perpetuate and extend it. Neither Celsus, Porphyry, nor Julian urged this as an objection to the New Testament; nor have the keen and sagacious enemies of Christianity in more modern times alleged that they have discovered that slavery was either originated by Christianity or that it lends its sanction to the system. If the question were submitted to any number of intelligent and impartial men whether the spirit of the New Testament is adverse to or favourable to slavery, and whether the fair application of the principles of the New Testament would perpetuate slavery or abolish it, it is presumed that on these points there would be no material difference of opinion. This conclusion would seem to be confirmed by the facts just adverted to,—that infidels have never made it an objection to the New Testament that it countenances or would perpetuate slavery, and that it is admitted, by even those who attempt to apologize for the system, that the fair application of Christianity would remove it from the world.*

2. The *general* course of the Christian church has been against slavery. This was undeniably true in the early history of the church. I know not that it has ever been alleged that any of the prominent defenders of the Christian faith among the 'fathers' were advocates of slavery, or that any decree of synods or councils can be adduced in favour of the system. The influence of Christianity, also, on slavery in the Roman empire is well known. Christianity *found* slavery everywhere ex-

* The only exception to these remarks which I recollect to have ever met with is the case of Professor Francis William Newman, in his work on the "Phases of Faith," in assigning his reasons for renouncing his early opinions and rejecting the Bible as a revelation. One of those reasons for his change of views (and the passage deserves to be quoted as illustrating and confirming the remark which I have made, that an appeal to the Bible as sustaining slavery tends to promote infidelity) is that the New Testament sanctions slavery, and is, in fact, the stronghold of those who defend the accursed system.

The passage in the "Phases of Faith" (pp. 166–167) in which this occurs is the following:—"Undue credit has been claimed for Christianity as the foe and extirpator of slavery. Englishmen of the nineteenth century boldly denounce slavery as an immoral and abominable system. There may be a little fanaticism in the fervour which this sometimes assumes; but not one of the Christian apostles ever opens his lips at all against slavery. Paul sent back the fugitive Onesimus to his master Philemon, with kind recommendations and apologies for the slave, but without a hint to the master that he ought to make him legally free. *At this day, in consequence, the New Testament is the argumentative stronghold of those in the United States who are trying to keep up the accursed system.*" For an answer to this, the reader may refer to the "Defence of the Eclipse of Faith," pp. 159, *et seq.*

isting; it introduced it nowhere. By a gradual but certain process it meliorated the system as it existed, and was among the most efficient causes of its being ultimately abolished in the Roman empire.* While there may have been a gradual tendency toward freedom in the opinions of the world, yet there can be no doubt that this was fostered, if not originated, by the prevalence of Christianity; and that when the time occurred, as it did, when slavery ceased to exist in what had been the Roman empire, one of the main causes which led to this was the silent influence of the Christian religion.

3. Efforts for emancipation have occurred usually in close connection with the Christian church, and under the influence of Christian men. The efforts which were made in England, and which resulted in emancipation throughout the British empire, were commenced and conducted under the influence of Christian men,—not of mere statesmen; not of infidels. Clarkson and Wilberforce and Buxton were Christian men; William Penn was a Christian; and all that has been done in the cause by the society of Friends has been originated by the fact that they regard the system as opposed to the gospel. Without any fear of contradiction, it may be affirmed that the efforts which have been made in the world to break the fetters of slavery; to suppress the slave-trade; and to give to all persons held in bondage the blessings of freedom, have been owing mainly to the influence of Christians,

* For proof of this I may be permitted to refer to my work on the "Scriptural Views of Slavery," pp. 368–372.

and that if it had not been for their influence those efforts would not have been made. The rejecters of the Bible have not been the movers in this cause; nor out of the church has there ever been enough power, under the mere promptings of humanity, to induce men to abandon the slave-traffic or to set the oppressed free. Whatever aid such men may have rendered to the cause, the moving power has always come originally from the bosom of the church:—from the silent influence of Christianity on the hearts of many men, or from the untiring energy, the tact, the eloquence, the self-denial, of some distinguished leader or leaders in the cause of emancipation, who have been made what they were by the power of the gospel of Christ.

4. It is true, also, that the great body of Christians in this land, and in all other lands, are opposed to slavery. It is not true that the authority of the best Christian writers can be adduced in favour of the system; nor is it true that the mass of Christians and of Christian ministers in the world are the advocates of slavery. A very large majority of Christians in this land own no slaves, and are, on principle, opposed to the owning of slaves. The whole number of slave-holders in the United States does not amount to four hundred thousand; and of these a small portion only are professors of religion. Not a few of those also who *are* slave-holders profess to be opposed to the system, and express a desire to be delivered from it. They see its evils and wrongs; they would not favour its introduction if it were not already in existence;

they endeavour to meliorate the condition of the slave; and they would sincerely rejoice if, consistently, as they suppose, with the best interests of the slaves themselves, they could all be made free. While they perceive difficulties in the way of emancipation, which to them appear insuperable at present, and which they see no prospect of being able soon to overcome, they feel the system to be a burden,—a burden to themselves, a burden to the slave. Not a few are so oppressed with this state of things that they leave the slave States, and emigrate to States where freedom prevails; and not a few more would, if we may credit their own testimony, rejoice if all that dwell in the land were free. The men who are connected with the church who openly advocate the system of slavery, and who would wish to make it perpetual, are comparatively few in number; and it is not a little remarkable that the apologists for slavery are not always those who are connected with the system, but men who sustain no relation to it whatever, and who voluntarily become advocates for a system which they who *are* connected with it regard as an unmitigated curse. Such men *deserve* no thanks from the world; and they *receive* no thanks from those who are suffering under the evils of the system, and who sigh for the day when they may be wholly delivered from it.

There is much indeed to lament in the feelings entertained in the church on the subject. There is much indifference to the evils of the system. There is much that pains the heart of philanthropy when we reflect how many there *are*, in the aggregate, in the church who apologize for the evil;

much to lament in the fact that there are *any* professed Christians who are holders of slaves. But, still, the church does not deserve unmitigated denunciation. The church, as such, is *not* the 'bulwark of slavery;' the church, as such, is not the advocate for slavery; the church, as such, is not the apologist for slavery. The whole society of Friends is detached from it, and their sentiments are well known to the world. One-half of the Methodist church in this country, and the whole of the Methodist denomination abroad, is opposed to slavery. All the branches, it is believed, of the Scotch church are opposed to the system. The German churches are equally opposed to it; the great body of Congregationalists are opposed to it, and their influence is that of decided hostility to it. The churches abroad—the Established church and the Dissenting churches in England; the two great bodies of the Presbyterian churches, and all the smaller bodies of Presbyterians in Scotland; the Presbyterians in Ireland, and *all* the churches on the Continent, so far as any expression of opinion has been made, are opposed to the system. Not a few of these foreign Christians, with entire propriety, utter a loud voice of remonstrance and appeal to their transatlantic brethren, and urge upon them, in language which cannot be misunderstood, the duty of detaching themselves entirely from the system, and assuming, in regard to it, the position occupied by the churches of other lands.

CHAPTER IV.

THE POSITION OF THE PRESBYTERIAN CHURCH BEFORE THE DIVISION, IN 1838, ON THE SUBJECT OF SLAVERY.

WITH these general remarks on the relation of the church to slavery, I proceed to consider more particularly the position of the Presbyterian church in regard to the system. The questions to be considered are:—What have been the expressed sentiments of that church on the subject? What is its position, according to the fair interpretation of the sentiments which it has expressed, in respect to it? What is the legitimate tendency or bearing of the measures which it has taken in regard to slavery? What would be the result if its own expressed principles were carried out? And what is the duty of that church, and of the church at large, on the subject?

A series of remarks will conduct us to correct conclusions in answer to these questions.

In the great division which occurred in 1838, the 'New-school' or 'Constitutional' Presbyterian church *inherited* the common sentiments of the whole Presbyterian church on this and on all other subjects. The 'New-school' body was not a *new* church with a new organization; but the one great church was 'divided' or '*split*' into two nearly equal parts, each portion of the great body inheriting the views, the doctrines, the influence, the '*prestige*,' of the whole.* The doc-

* This is the doctrine laid down on the subject by the Supreme Court of Pennsylvania. The exact legal relation of the two branches of the Presbyterian church will be seen from the decision in the case of The Presbyterian Congregation *vs*. Johnston, as laid down by Chief-Justice Gibson. It is as follows:—[The italics and small capitals are mine.]

"Now, since the foundation of this congregation an event has happened which the founders did not contemplate, and which would not have been provided for had it been foreseen. This was no less than a dismemberment of the Presbyterian body, not indeed by disorganization of it or an entire reduction of it to its primitive elements, but by an excision, constitutional though it was, of whole synods with their presbyteries and congregations. There was not merely a secession of particles, leaving the original mass entire, *but the original mass was* SPLIT *into two fragments of nearly equal magnitude;* and, though it was held by this court, in The Commonwealth *vs*. Green, 5 Whart. Rep, 531, that the party which *happened* to be in office by means of its numerical superiority at the time of the division was that which was entitled to represent it and perform the functions of the original body, it was not *because the minority were thought to be any thing else than Presbyterians*, but because a popular body is known only by its government or head.

"That they differed from the majority *in doctrine or discipline* was not pretended, though it was alleged that they did not maintain the scriptural warrant of ruling elders. But the difference in this respect had been tolerated if not sanctioned by the Assembly itself, which, with full knowledge of it, had allowed the heterodox synods to grow up as part of the church, and it could not therefore have been viewed as radical or essential.

"We were called on, however, to pass, not on a question of heresy, for we would have been incompetent to decide it, but on the regularity of the meeting at which the trustees were chosen. I mention this to show that we did not determine that the excision was expurgation, and not division. Indeed, the measure would seem to have been as decisively REVOLUTIONARY as would be an exclusion of particular States from the Federal Union for the adoption of an anti-republican form of government. The excluded synods, gathering to themselves

trines of the one great body became the doctrines of both; the history of the one was the history of both; the names that had given lustre to the Presbyterian denomination in this land became names common to the history of both; the influence which the Presbyterian church had exerted in the promotion of education, liberty, and learning, in the founding of colleges, seminaries, and schools, in the establishment of American freedom, in planting churches in the wilderness, and in sending the gospel to heathen tribes, became the common inheritance of both. These things could not be divided. They could not be appropriated, in whole or in part, exclusively by either of the two great branches of the church. Property could be appropriated by one of the parties; and it was. Seminaries of learning, richly

---

the disaffected in other quarters of the church, formed themselves into a distinct body, governed by a supreme judicatory, *so like its fellow as to pass for its twin-brother*, and even to lay claim to the succession. That the Old-school party succeeded to the privileges and property of the Assembly was not *because it was more Presbyterian than the other*, BUT BECAUSE IT WAS STRONGER; for, had it been the weaker, it would have been the party excluded, and the New-school party, exercising the government as it then had done, would have succeeded in its stead; and thus the doctrine pressed upon us would have made title to church-property the sport of accident. In that event, an attempt to deprive the Old-school congregations of their churches, for an act of the majority in withdrawing from the jurisdiction of the Assembly, would have loaded the New-school party with such a weight of popular odium as would have sunk it. Here then was *the original mass divided into two parts of nearly equal magnitude and similar structure;* and what was a congregation in the predicament of the one before us to do? It surely was not bound to follow the party which was successful in the conflict merely because superiority of numbers had given it the victory."—1 *Watts and Sergeant's Reports*, p. 9, per Gibson, in delivering the opinion of the court, p. 38.

endowed by the common toils and sacrifices of the whole church, could be appropriated by one of the parties; and they were. Professorships, scholarships, libraries, edifices reared for sacred learning, and funds collected for the common use of the whole church, could thus be diverted from their original purpose and be made to subserve the interests of a part; and they were thus diverted. But it was not thus with the '*prestige*' of the Presbyterian name; not thus with the recorded virtues of the earlier labourers in the ministry; not thus with the influence that had gone out from the schools and colleges founded for the use of the common church; not thus with the history of the revivals of religion with which God had blessed the earlier labourers in the great denomination. Whatever there was or is in the fame of the Tennents, of Davies, of Witherspoon, that has contributed to promote sound learning and pure religion, or to make the church respected at home and honoured abroad, pertained alike to both. Up to the year 1838, the men who have presided over the General Assembly of the church belong to both divisions of the church; and they who stand by the graves of the Tennents, of Davies, or of Witherspoon, be they Old or New-school, have a common interest in their honoured names, and in the work which they did for promoting the cause of religion in the land. Property, though held in trust for common sacred uses, may be appropriated to the purposes of a party, but the fame of a common ancestry belongs to all; and, whatever *disposition* there might be to appropriate *that* also, God has so constructed society that that is incapable of being plundered or of being made to subserve the ends of schism, injustice, or revolution.

As a part of this rich inheritance, the 'New-school' portion of the Presbyterian church received, in common with the division now called the 'Old-school,' the recorded testimonies of the church on the subject of slavery. Up to the time of the division in 1838, the 'New-school' body is to be regarded as holding the same sentiment as the 'Old,'—the common sentiment of the whole church. From that time the two branches into which the whole church was divided have taken each their own position before the world. The one has endeavoured to carry out, by a proper application to the subject, the principles avowed before by the whole body and which were the common inheritance of both; the other has endeavoured to *arrest* the progress of opinion, to check all advances, to avoid all the proper application of those principles; and, so far as appears, to make slavery a permanent institution in the church. It is proper, therefore, now to inquire what *was* the position of the Presbyterian church before the division, on the subject.

At a very early period in the history of this country the attention of the Presbyterian church was directed to the subject of slavery, and the firm conviction of that church in regard to the evil of the system, and the desirableness of universal emancipation, was expressed without any ambiguity.

Thus, before the General Assembly was constituted, the Synod of New York and Philadelphia, in the year 1787, adopted the following resolutions:—

"The Synod of New York and Philadelphia do highly approve of the general principles, in favour of universal liberty, that prevail in America, and of the interest which many of the States have taken in promoting the abolition of slavery; yet, inasmuch as men, introduced from a servile state to a participation of all the privileges of civil society without a proper education and without previous habits of industry, may be, in many respects, dangerous to the community: Therefore, they earnestly recommend it to all the members belonging to their communion to give those persons who are at present held in servitude such good education as may prepare them for the better enjoyment of freedom. And they, moreover, recommend that masters, whenever they find servants disposed to make a proper improvement of the privilege, would give them some share of property to begin with, or grant them sufficient time and sufficient means of procuring by industry their own liberty at a moderate rate; that they may thereby be brought into society with those habits of industry that may render them useful citizens:—and, finally, they recommend it to all the people under their care to use the most prudent measures, consistent with the interest and the state of civil society in the parts where they live, to procure, eventually, the final abolition of slavery in America."

In the year 1818, the General Assembly adopted the following remarkable and well-known resolutions with entire unanimity:—

"The General Assembly of the Presbyterian church, having taken into consideration the subject of SLAVERY, think proper to make known their sentiments upon it to the churches and people under their care.

"We consider the voluntary enslaving of one part of the human race by another as a gross violation of the most precious and sacred rights of human nature, as utterly inconsistent with the law of God which requires us to love our neighbour as ourselves, and as totally irreconcilable with the spirit and principles of the gospel of Christ, which enjoin that 'all things whatsoever ye would that men should do to you, do ye even so to them.' Slavery creates a paradox in the moral system; it exhibits rational, accountable, and immortal beings in such circumstances as scarcely to leave them the power of moral action. It exhibits them as dependent on the will of others whether they shall receive religious instruction; whether they shall know and worship the true God; whether they shall enjoy the ordinances of the gospel; whether they shall perform the duties and cherish the endearments of husbands and wives, parents and children, neighbours and friends; whether they shall preserve their chastity and purity, or regard the dictates of justice and humanity. Such are some of the consequences of slavery,—consequences not imaginary, but which connect themselves with its very existence. The evils to which the slave is *always* exposed often take place in fact and in their very worst degree and form; and where all of them do not take place, as we rejoice to say that in many instances, through the influence of the principles of humanity and religion on the minds of masters, they do not, still, the slave is deprived of his natural right, degraded as a human being, and exposed to the danger of passing into the hands of a master who may inflict upon him all the hardships and injuries which inhumanity and avarice may suggest.

"From this view of the consequences, resulting from the practice into which Christian people have most inconsistently fallen, of enslaving a portion of their *brethren* of mankind,—for 'God hath made of one blood all nations of men to dwell on the face of the earth,'—it is manifestly the duty of all Christians who enjoy the light of the present day, when the inconsistency of slavery, both with the dictates of humanity and religion, has been demonstrated, and is generally seen and acknowledged, to use their honest, earnest, and unwearied endeavours to correct the errors of former times, and as speedily as possible to efface this blot on our holy religion, and to obtain the complete abolition of slavery throughout Christendom, and if possible throughout the world.

"We rejoice that the church to which we belong commenced, as early as any other in this country, the good work of endeavouring to put an end to slavery, and that in the same work many of its members have ever since been, and now are, among the most active, vigorous, and efficient labourers. We do, indeed, tenderly sympathize with those portions of our church and our country where the evil of slavery has been entailed upon them; where a *great*, and *the most virtuous, part* of the *community* abhor slavery, and wish its extermination as sincerely as any others; but where the number of slaves, their ignorance, and their vicious habits generally, render an immediate and universal emancipation inconsistent alike with the safety and happiness of the master and the slave. With those who are thus circumstanced, we repeat that we tenderly sympathize. At the same time, we earnestly exhort them to continue, and, if possible, to increase, their exertions TO EFFECT A TOTAL ABOLITION OF SLAVERY. We exhort them to suffer no greater delay to take place in this most interesting concern than a regard to the public welfare *truly* and *indispensably* demands.

"*The manifest violation or disregard of the injunction here given, in its true spirit and intention, ought to be considered as just ground for the discipline and censures of the church. And if it shall ever happen that a Christian professor, in our communion, shall sell a slave who is also in communion and good standing with our church, contrary to his or her will and inclination, it ought immediately to claim the particular attention of the proper church judicature; and, unless there be such peculiar circumstances attending the case as can but seldom happen, it ought to be followed, without delay, by a suspension of the offender from all the privileges of the church till he repent and make all the reparation in his power to the injured party.*"

Respecting this document, as showing what is the real position of the Presbyterian church on the subject of slavery, I make the following remarks:—

1. It was quite in accordance with the prevalent conviction at that time in regard to slavery. The language employed is perhaps stronger than that which was commonly used; but the general sentiment is to be regarded as in accordance with the prevailing opinion of the time. So far as appears, the document had the unanimous approval of the committee who reported it; and it is expressly stated (Minutes, p. 28) that it was 'unanimously adopted' by the Assembly. It does not appear even to have excited any opposition in debate; nor is there any evidence that the sentiments embodied in the paper gave rise to any discussion. There is no evidence that it met with any opposition from any part of the church after the adjournment of the Assembly; but it seems to have been as unanimously acquiesced in by the church at large as it had been by the Assembly. No presbytery or synod took action against it; no church uttered a word of remonstrance. It was received as expressing the settled convictions of the church on the subject; it was recorded in the minutes of the Assembly as a document too important to be disposed of by merely placing it on file; it was subsequently published in the 'Digest' of the Assembly as among the documents most important to be preserved and diffused through the church; it has never been changed or modified, in a period of nearly forty years, either by the church when united or by either body since the division. It went forth to the world as expressing

the unanimous conviction of the North and the South as represented in the Assembly on the subject, and with all the influence which could be given to a document from the name of the chairman of the committee who drafted it, and who, and for a quarter of a century afterward, exerted more influence in the Presbyterian church than any other man then living. It is the calm, deliberate, unanimous sentiment of a grave body of Christian men representing the North and the South, and uttering a decided Christian conviction on the subject at a time when men had not learned to apologize for the evil, or to dilute and weaken a testimony against it by great zeal for the 'Union,' and by endeavouring to make a merit of 'conservatism.'

2. These resolutions put the Presbyterian church on an elevated and honourable position in regard to the evil of slavery. It was a position then unoccupied by any other denomination of Christians except the society of Friends; and, in respect to the clearness and firmness of the expressions respecting the evils of slavery, it was not surpassed by any of the declarations which had ever issued from that body. It is claimed in the very resolutions themselves, as a matter of felicitation, that the Presbyterian church had been among the foremost in bearing its testimony against slavery and in taking measures which contemplated its entire abolition. Thus, the committee say, "We *rejoice* that the church to which we belong commenced, *as early as any other in the country*, the good work of PUTTING AN END TO SLAVERY." It was then no dishonour to be regarded as *first* in the work of universal emancipation; it was no dis-

honour to institute measures contemplating the ultimate removal of slavery from the land and world.

3. The resolutions of the Assembly contemplated the entire removal of slavery, and are such as would now be charged with radical abolitionism. There is not one word of apology for the system; there is no attempt made to show that it is a 'patriarchal' institution; there is no appeal to the Bible as originating or sustaining it; there is no hint that the apostles placed the relation of 'master and servant' on the same basis as the relation of parent and child, master and apprentice, guardian and ward; there is no intimation that the system is to be perpetual in the church or in the world; there is no saving clause in favour of the relation itself, while the *abuses* of the system only are attacked; there is the most decided, absolute, and unqualified condemnation *of the system itself*, as evil, and only evil,—a system fraught with nothing but evil,—a system to be abolished as soon as it could be done. Thus, the Assembly says, "We regard the voluntary enslaving of one part of the human race by another *as a gross violation of the most precious and sacred rights of human nature, as utterly inconsistent with the law of God, and as totally irreconcilable with the spirit and principles of the gospel of Christ.*" Again, they say, "It is manifestly the duty of all Christians who enjoy the light of the present day, to use their honest, earnest, and unwearied endeavours AS SPEEDILY AS POSSIBLE *to efface this blot on our holy religion, and to obtain the* COMPLETE ABOLITION of slavery *throughout Christendom, and, if possible, throughout the world.*" So, again, they speak of their desire that all suitable

exertion should be made "TO EFFECT A TOTAL ABOLITION OF SLAVERY." So, again, they speak of "*the duty indisputably incumbent on all Christians to labour for* ITS COMPLETE EXTINCTION."

This language looks to the entire extinction of slavery—the complete emancipation of every slave—as the end to be contemplated; and the purpose expressed by the Assembly could *not* be carried out except by universal emancipation. The aim, the tendency, the object, is *abolitionism;* and the Assembly of 1818 was to all intents and purposes an abolition Assembly. An assemblage of men in the Presbyterian church, or in any other church, or unconnected with any church, which should now adopt the same resolutions, would be characterized and would be extensively denounced as an abolition body; and if perchance there were members in such an assemblage from the slave-holding States, they would regard it as their duty to protest against such doctrines; to write soothing letters to their churches, expressing their dissent from these doctrines, and apologizing for their remaining in connection with a body of men which held and promulgated such views. In neither branch of the Presbyterian church—perhaps in almost no other church in the land—could such resolutions now be carried unanimously, or carried at all without solemn protests and warnings against the exciting and disorganizing tendencies of such doctrines. Yet these are the solemn, recorded, unrepealed, and unmodified doctrines of the Presbyterian church, Old-school and New, on the subject of slavery. These sentiments have been before the world for nearly forty years as the doctrine of the church on the subject. These are the principles which are now professedly held by both branches of the Presbyterian church. These, till repealed, constitute *a proper basis* for any action on the subject of slavery; and these would lead to, and would justify, a continued agitation of the subject until the conscience of the church should be so reached as wholly to detach itself from all connection with the system. The existence of slavery in the church is INCONSISTENT with these avowed principles; and consistency in either body will never be secured until these principles are carried out by universal emancipation.

4. According to the principles involved in these papers of the Assembly, the holding of slaves is presumptive evidence of a man's not being in good standing in the church. That is, he cannot be contemplated as in the same position in this respect as the man who sustains the relation of parent or husband, or as the master of an apprentice. There is an implied censure—an expression of condemnation—on the man who sustains this relation. If he is to be regarded as in good standing,—as acting in that relation consistently with the Christian character,—it is for him to make out the case by showing that he sustains this relation by the necessity of the case; that he does not hold his slaves as property for the purpose of sale; that he is making all reasonable and practicable efforts for their emancipation; that he contemplates their freedom, and that he is willing to avail himself of any practicable method of promoting it. A man who sustains the relation of parent, or husband, or master of an

apprentice, is, so far as these relations are concerned, presumed to be in good standing in the church. There is, there can be, no presumption against it from this relation. In these resolutions of the Assembly there is no denunciation of the evils of those relations; no implication that there are any evils in those relations; no exhortation to bring those relations to an end. But the reference to slavery is of an entirely different character. How *can* he be regarded as in good standing in the church, in the same sense as in these relations, who is acting under a system, and is a participator in and a practical supporter of a system, which is declared to be "*a gross violation of the most precious and sacred rights of human nature, as utterly inconsistent with the law of God, and as* TOTALLY *irreconcilable with the spirit and principles of the gospel of Christ*"? Suppose these things to be affirmed of a man in any other respect: suppose that in reference to his commercial employments, or his profession, or his mode of living, or his domestic relations, it were affirmed of him that he was habitually acting in a way which was "a gross violation of the most precious and sacred rights of human nature, which was utterly inconsistent with the law of God, and which was totally irreconcilable with the spirit and principles of the gospel of Christ," assuredly his good standing in the church would not be a thing to be *assumed* as unquestioned as if this were of course consistent with the Christian character, but as a thing *to be made out*, if it could be, by denying the truth of this accusation, or by showing that the conduct charged on him, in the circumstances of the case, was so *necessary* as to make it consistent with the Christian name,—if that could be done. But suppose that he contemplated this as a permanent and established course of life: would the presumption be that his standing in the church was such that it could not with propriety be called in question, or would it be otherwise?

We are led to the same view of the matter by the statement in these resolutions, that "it is manifestly the duty of *all* Christians who enjoy the light of the present day, when the inconsistency of slavery both with the dictates of humanity and religion has been demonstrated, and is generally seen and acknowledged, to use their honest, earnest, and unwearied endeavours as *speedily as possible to efface this blot on our holy religion, and to obtain the complete abolition of slavery throughout Christendom, and, if possible, throughout the world.*" Can it be supposed that a man who did *not* make this effort,—who intended to maintain a course of life which was declared to be "irreconcilable with the spirit and principles of the gospel of Christ,"—who intended to do all that he could to perpetuate a relation which was declared to be a "blot on our holy religion,"—or who in his own mind placed such a relation on the same basis as that of parent and child, master and apprentice, and ruler and subject,—was to be regarded as presumptively in good standing in the church? What kind of a church would that be which should admit such a principle as this? Who would wish to join it? Who would deem himself honoured by a connection with it? And how far would such a *church* differ from a horde of banditti or an association of gamblers or pirates? Of *such* an association what more could be said than was said by the Assembly of 1818 of slavery? And can it be believed that the Assembly which adopted these resolutions, and the Assemblies which have since given their sanction to them, *meant* to teach that a man who, of design and purpose, lent his own active co-operation to perpetuate a system which has been demonstrated and is generally seen and acknowledged to be 'inconsistent both with the dictates of humanity and religion,' and which is '*a blot on our holy religion*,' to be regarded as in good and regular standing in the church of Christ?

5. It is clear, from these resolutions, that, in the apprehension of that Assembly, slave-holding *may* become a proper subject of discipline in the church. Thus, the resolutions affirm that, "if it shall ever happen that a Christian professor, in our communion, shall sell a slave who is also in communion and good standing in our church, contrary to his or her will and inclination, it ought immediately to claim the particular attention of the proper church judicature; and, unless there be such peculiar circumstances attending the case as can but seldom happen, it ought to be followed, without delay, by a suspension of the offender from all the privileges of the church till he repent and make all the reparation in his power to the injured party."* It is, indeed, to be regretted that the Assembly did not include *every* case of selling a slave, whether a member of the church or not, and that a distinction should have been even *implied* in regard to those who are and those who are not

* Minutes of the Assembly of 1818, p. 33.

members of the church,—as if that might be proper treatment toward one which would be sin against the other; but, still, the declaration is explicit that an act which is not uncommon in all slave States, and which may occur under the system anywhere, is a proper subject for discipline in the church, and should exclude from its communion. So the Assembly says, "The manifest violation or disregard of the injunction here given"—the injunction to secure the kind 'treatment of slaves,' forbidding the 'separation of husband and wife,' and 'selling slaves to those who will deprive them of the blessings of the gospel, or transport them to places where the gospel is not proclaimed, or where it is forbidden to slaves to attend upon its institutions'—"ought to be considered just ground for the discipline and censures of the church:" (p. 33.) And, moreover, is it not fairly implied, in these resolutions of the Assembly, that the act of slave-holding, unless it can be made out to be a case of necessity or humanity, may properly be regarded as a subject of discipline in the church? Can any man doubt that to pursue systematically and voluntarily any course of life, or to engage in any business, or to sustain any relation, either of which is 'a gross violation of the most precious and sacred rights of human nature, which is utterly inconsistent with the law of God, which is totally irreconcilable with the spirit and principles of the gospel of Christ, and which is a blot on our holy religion,' should subject an offender to the discipline of the church? What *are* proper subjects of discipline, if these things are not? Where is the line to be drawn, if conduct such as this is not to be classed with 'offences'? What may *not* exempt a man from the censures of the church, and from the exercise of its discipline, if such a course of life is to be regarded as exempt?

Such are some of the things implied in this remarkable act of the Assembly of the Presbyterian church. These resolutions have never been repealed by any act of the entire church when united, or by any act of either of the branches of the church since the division. Their propriety has never, by any public act, been called in question. They stand upon the records of the Presbyterian church; they have been published in the 'Digests' containing documents regarded as of peculiar value; they have been sent abroad to the world; they *committed* the Presbyterian church to a well-defined course of policy and action. They belong, as the common inheritance, to both branches of the church. Whatever merit they may claim belongs to both those branches; whatever obloquy they may be supposed to deserve belongs to one as much as to the other. Both branches of the church are COMMITTED to these views, and to whatever course of policy they may legitimately lead on this great subject.

CHAPTER V.

THE POSITION OF THE 'NEW-SCHOOL' OR 'CONSTITUTIONAL' PRESBYTERIAN CHURCH ON THE SUBJECT OF SLAVERY.

It is not my design to inquire whether the 'Old-school' have or have not been true to the resolutions of the Act of Assembly of 1818, and have taken the position before the world to which those resolutions would prompt; nor is it my design to inquire whether the state of feeling in *that* branch of the church is of such a nature that those resolutions *could* now be adopted, or of such a nature that they would be a fair exponent of the views entertained in that branch of the church. With all kindness of feeling toward that denomination of Christians, it must be regarded by any reflecting man as a subject of felicitation that he is not called on to vindicate the course pursued by that body on many other subjects than that of slavery, and that he is in circumstances to make him in no wise responsible for many of their public acts. How long those resolutions shall be suffered to lie unnoticed in their minutes; how long it may be possible to stifle the feelings which, it is to be hoped, still linger in some portions of that body; how long it may be consistent to repress all discussion in reference to evils so solemnly denounced, and which have in no wise been diminished since the adoption of these resolutions; how long it may be proper for a large body of Christians to slumber over this stupendous evil, never even lifting a note of remonstrance or appeal on the subject, it is for them, subject to their responsibility to God, to decide.

Leaving that as a matter in no way pertaining to the portion of the church which they have separated from themselves, I propose now to show that the action of the New-school branch of the church is such as to evince, in good faith, a purpose to carry out those resolutions, and to secure, by all proper and constitutional means, the end contemplated by them;—"as speedily as possible to efface this blot on our holy religion, and to obtain the complete abolition of slavery throughout Christendom, and, if possible, throughout the world;" or, in other words, that all the acts of that body on the subject are but a development of the principles involved in those resolutions.

In reference to this, and as showing the true position of the 'New-school' Presbyterian church on the subject, I would make the following remarks:—

1. The subject has been most freely *discussed* in the New-school General Assembly. No one subject, from the time of the division of the church in 1838, has been so frequently before the Assembly; no one has been discussed more freely; no one has called forth more entirely whatever wisdom there might be in the General Assembly to lead to some satisfactory result. If there has been at any time, and from any quarters, a disposition to suppress discussion and action, it has been resisted by a strong

and unambiguous voice of the church demanding that the subject should *not* be suppressed; if in any of the meetings of the Assembly from that time to the present it has been judged *not* proper then to discuss this subject, that course has been taken, not because it was the conviction of the church that the subject should *not* be discussed, but either because at that time some other subject seemed more particularly to demand the attention of the Assembly, or because it was not apparent that any other step could be taken in advance of points which had been already gained. In these discussions, continued now for nearly twenty years, every part of the church has been fully heard; every facility has been given for the fullest expression of opinion. The advocates of slavery—of whom there have been *very* few—have been heard with all the patience that they could desire; and the members of the Assembly who have come from those portions of the church where slavery prevails have heard the system denounced, and have listened to arguments to prove that it is contrary to the Bible and fraught with innumerable evils to the bodies and souls of men, with a candour, a degree of patience, and a measure of Christian forbearance, which has greatly commended them to the confidence of their brethren; which has shown that *they* were not insensible to the evils of the system; and which has shown that, while they could not agree with their brethren in sentiment, they could not be surpassed by them in Christian courtesy. The great principle was soon thoroughly settled after the division of the church, that, in the New-school portion of that body, the subject of slavery *might* be, and *ought* to be, discussed. At a time when there was every possible effort made to keep the subject out of the houses of Congress; at a time when it was, in fact, excluded from nearly every other ecclesiastical body in the land,—the Methodist church being almost the only exception; at a time when Episcopalians, and Baptists, and Old-school Presbyterians, gloried that their churches were kept prudently and conservatively free from the intrusion of the agitating topic; and at a time when not a few of the 'Old-school' body apparently hoped to make 'capital' from the agitation of this subject by the portion of the church which they had 'excluded,' and when they watched with the keen, observing eye of prospective gain to have the New-school body fall to pieces under the discussion, and when they hoped to augment their own strength by attracting to themselves the scattered fragments of the dissevered body; —at that very time, and in view of all these perils, and under all the disadvantages of an imperfect organization, the example has been set, year after year, in the General Assemblies of the New-school, of a most free, full, candid, and patient discussion of this agitating subject. Not a presbytery, not a church, not a man, as far as is known, North or South, has left the church in consequence of the discussion; and, if they who from without have watched the discussion with the interest which men feel who are encouraged to hope that they will augment their own numbers by the divisions which occur in other bodies, never has there been an instance of more signal disappointment than has occurred in this case. I state this, then, in relation to the actual position of the New-school body on this subject, that it is a point gained, and is not to be receded from, that the subject of slavery may be discussed in the church to any extent which may be thought desirable; and that, in fact, there is no other denomination of Christians in the land, not even the Congregational, where the subject has been so freely examined, or has called forth so much prayer and solicitude as to the course which should be pursued by the church. In this respect—in an honest effort to know what is true and right, to understand the real bearings of the system, to ascertain what is the exact power of the church in regard to the system—the New-school Presbyterian church is in advance of all the other churches of the land. It has freely discussed a subject which it has been the boasted wisdom of others thus far to exclude from their councils; it has frankly and fearlessly grappled with difficulties which *they all have yet to meet.*

2. It is true, also, in regard to the New-school Presbyterian church, that in all the discussions which have been had on slavery, and in all the resolutions which have been adopted, the Act of 1818 has neither been repealed, nor has there been any attempt to repeal it, nor has the propriety of the sentiments contained in it ever been called in question. Not even in debate, it is believed, has the idea ever been advanced that the resolutions in that act did not, at the time of its adoption, fairly represent the opinions of the whole Presbyterian church, or that, since the division, they did not fairly express the views and define the position of the New-school portion of the church on the subject of slavery. Those reso-

lutions are an inherited and an unrepealed part of the declared sentiments of the Presbyterian church; and any action which would be a legitimate carrying out of these principles must be regarded as unquestionably proper.

3. The course pursued in the New-school portion of the church, since the division, has been but the proper carrying out of the principles involved in these resolutions, and has been, I may perhaps be able to show, all that could be done, as yet, under the constitution of the church. To show this, it may be proper to recall the successive steps in the action of the General Assembly, and then to inquire whether this does not indicate PROGRESS,—and, under the circumstances of the case, all the progress which up to the present time could be made in carrying out the resolutions of 1818.

In 1839—the year after the division of the church—the General Assembly of the New-school portion of the church, after a full discussion of the subject, adopted the following resolution:—"Whereas, certain memorials have been sent up to this Assembly from several presbyteries, desiring some action on the subject of *slavery;* and whereas these memorials have been read and freely discussed by this body; and whereas this Assembly is made up of members from different portions of our extended country, who honestly differ in opinion as well in regard to the propriety as the nature of the ecclesiastical action desired in the case: therefore, Resolved, That this Assembly does most solemnly refer to the lower judicatories the subject of slavery, leaving it to them to take such order thereon as in their judgment will be the most judicious and *adapted to remove the evil.*" (Minutes of the Assembly for 1839, p. 22.)

The following things are to be noticed in regard to this resolution.

(*a*) It indicates an early purpose on the part of the church to consider the subject of slavery. But one year after the separation, while the church could as yet be scarcely regarded as organized, with all the perplexities and responsibilities of the pending law-suit with the other portion of the church, with all that there might be in the circumstances of the church at that time that might seem to make it expedient not to agitate the subject of slavery, and with all the predictions that an agitation of the subject would again rend and divide the church, this subject was taken up as one of the most important that had a claim on the attention of the church, and in such a manner as to indicate a determined purpose to assume a right position on the subject, whatever might be the consequences to the church itself.

(*b*) A course was pursued which was strictly Presbyterian and strictly proper. It was to refer the matter to 'the lower judicatories,'—meaning particularly, undoubtedly, the synods, presbyteries, and sessions in the portion of our country where slavery exists. It was felt that the matter pertained primarily to them; that the proper action should begin with them; that the subject was one in which they had a special interest, and which it was supposed they would be best qualified to understand; and it was presumed that they *would* take such 'action' in the case as might prevent the necessity of bringing the matter again before the General Assembly, or make it a subject of general agitation in the church. But, whatever might be the result,—whatever might be the disposition of the 'lower judicatories'—the sessions, presbyteries, and synods—in regard to the matter,—it was clearly in accordance with the Constitution of the church, and with Christian propriety, that the subject *should* be referred to them in the first instance, in order that they might in a regular and constitutional way endeavour to carry out the principles of the church on the subject, and devise some efficient method for detaching the church from all connection with slavery.

(*c*) The subject that was left to the 'lower judicatories' was perfectly defined. It was, in the words of the resolution, to "take such *action* as, in their judgment, would be most judicious *and best adapted to* REMOVE THE EVIL." *The removal of the evil*—in other words, in the language of the resolutions of 1818, "*the entire abolition of slavery*"—was the end contemplated, and the only end. To this end, and this alone, in a proper and judicious manner, the attention of the 'lower judicatories' was directed. There is no suggestion that the institution is designed to be permanent; no intimation that it is a 'patriarchal' institution, or that it is an institution that is in any way sanctioned and sustained by the Bible; no hint that it is on the same level as the relation of husband and wife, or parent and child:—it is an '*evil;*' an evil not to be perpetuated, but 'REMOVED.' This was undoubtedly the view of the Assembly in 1839,—the earliest period in which the New-school Assembly could act on the subject, or in which it could declare the views of the church.

In the General Assembly of 1840, the subject of

slavery was again introduced, and occupied a considerable part of four days of the session, and was then, apparently in view of the action of the previous Assembly, and the difficulty of agreeing on any new measure better adapted to "remove the evil," indefinitely postponed. The fact, however, that the subject occupied so large a portion of the time of the Assembly, shows that it was one which excited deep interest in the church, and was one which the Assembly was not disposed to exclude from solemn and anxious consideration.

The New-school Assembly, then triennial, met again in 1843. The subject again occupied the attention of the Assembly for a considerable part of three days of the session. After a full discussion, the Assembly adopted the following resolution:— "Whereas, there is in this Assembly great diversity of opinion as to the proper and best mode of action on the subject of slavery; and whereas, in such circumstances, any expression of sentiment would carry with it but little weight, as it would be passed by a small majority and must operate to produce alienation and division; and whereas the Assembly of 1839, with great unanimity, referred this whole subject to the lower judicatories, to take such order as in their judgment might be adopted to remove the evil:

"Resolved, That the Assembly do not think it for the edification of the church, for their body to take any action on the subject." (Minutes of the Assembly for 1843, pp. 18, 19.)

It is necessary to remark only on this action of the Assembly,—

(*a*) That the fact that the subject was again so fully

discussed shows the deep interest which the church took in the subject.

(*b*) That the same object was contemplated which had been avowed in 1818,—the 'entire abolition' of slavery in the church:—"Such order as in their judgment might *be adapted to remove the evil*,"—not the '*evils*' of slavery, or the abuses of the system, but the '*evil*' itself, or the system as *evil*.

(*c*) *This* judgment of the Assembly seems to have been decided and harmonious; as no one, amidst the diversity of views about the proper mode of reaching the evil, even seems to have called in question the fact that it was an evil, and an evil '*to be removed.*'

The General Assembly again met in 1846, and took still more decided action in regard to slavery, showing what was the prevalent feeling on the subject in the church, and indicating decided *progress* in the development of the principles before laid down. In that year they adopted, by a vote of ninety-two to twenty-nine, the following important paper:—

"1. The system of slavery, as it exists in these United States, viewed either in the laws of the several States which sanction it, or in its actual operation and results in society, is intrinsically an unrighteous and oppressive system, and is opposed to the prescriptions of the law of God, to the spirit and precepts of the gospel, and to the best interests of humanity.

"2. The testimony of the General Assembly, from A.D. 1787 to 1818, inclusive, has condemned it; and it remains still the recorded testimony of the Presbyterian church of these United States against it, from which we do not recede.

"3. We cannot therefore withhold the expression of our deep regret that slavery should be continued and countenanced by any of the members of our churches; and we do earnestly exhort both them, and the churches among whom it exists, to use all means in their power to put it away from them. Its perpetuation among them cannot fail to be regarded by multitudes, influenced by their example, as sanctioning the system portrayed in and maintained by the statutes of the several slave-holding States wherein they dwell. Nor can any mere mitigation of its severity, prompted by the humanity and Christian feelings of any individuals who continue to hold their fellow-men in such bondage, be regarded either as a testimony against the system, or as in the least degree changing its essential character.

"4. But, while we believe that many evils, incident to the system, render it important and obligatory to bear testimony against it, yet would we not undertake to determine the degree of moral turpitude on the part of individuals involved by it. This will doubtless be found to vary in the sight of God, according to the degree of light and other circumstances pertaining to each. In view of all the embarrassments and obstacles in the way of emancipation interposed by the statutes of the slave-holding States, and by the social influence affecting the views and conduct of those involved in it, we cannot pronounce a judgment of general and promiscuous condemnation, implying that destitution of Christian principle and feeling which should exclude from the table of the Lord all who stand in the legal relation of masters to slaves, or justify us in withholding our ecclesiastical and Christian fellowship from them. We rather sympathize with and would seek to succour them in their embarrassments, believing that separation and secession among the churches and their members are not the methods that God approves and sanctions for the reformation of his church.

"5. While, therefore, we feel bound to bear our testimony against slavery, and to exhort our beloved brethren to remove it from them as speedily as possible, by all appropriate and available means, we do at the same time condemn all divisive and schismatical measures tending to destroy the unity and disturb the peace of our churches, and deprecate the spirit of denunciation, and that unfeeling severity which would cast from the fold those whom we are rather bound, by the spirit of the gospel and the obligations of our covenant, to instruct, to counsel, exhort, and try to lead in the ways of God, and toward whom, even though they may err, to exercise forbearance and brotherly love.

"6. As a court of our Lord Jesus Christ, we possess no legislative authority; and as the General Assembly of the Presbyterian Church, we possess no judiciary authority. We have no right to institute and prescribe tests of Christian character and church-membership not recognised and sanctioned in the Sacred Scriptures and in our standards, by which we have agreed to walk. We must, therefore, leave this matter with the sessions, and presbyteries, and synods,—the judicatories to whom pertains the right of judgment,—to act in the administration of discipline as they may judge it to be their duty, constitutionally subject to the General Assembly only in the way of general review and control."

Of this important paper it seems proper to make the following remarks.

(*a*) It was adopted after the most free and full discussion that this subject, or perhaps any other, had ever had in the General Assembly. At an early period of the session of the Assembly it was resolved, in order to give the fullest opportunity for an expression of opinion, that the roll be called, "that each member may have an opportunity of expressing his opinion on the general subject." (Minutes, p. 15.) From the minutes of the Assembly it appears that the subject occupied the attention of the Assembly, almost to the exclusion of every other subject, for *twelve* sessions of the Assembly that year, and they who were present on that occasion know well that the most ample range was given in the debate, and that the most free opportunity was allowed for an expression of opinion. There has been no ecclesiastical meeting in our country where the subject of slavery has received so full a discussion, or where so large a portion of its time has been occupied in considering the subject. It is probable, indeed, that the subject has *never* in this country received so full a discussion as it did in that Assembly. It will be remembered, also, that though an *earnest* it was not an *angry* discussion; and though, of course, there was diversity of opinion, yet there was no rupture of the church, or alienation of feeling, as the result of the discussion.

(*b*) The resolutions affirm and adopt the previous action of the Assembly as expressing the views then entertained on the subject. Particularly the resolutions affirm that the "testimony of the General Assembly from 1787 to 1818 remains still the recorded testimony of the Presbyterian church in these United States against it, *from which we do not recede.*"

(*c*) The resolutions of the Assembly of 1846 are but a proper *development* of the principles before laid down and affirmed by the Presbyterian church. There is nothing, it is presumed it will be admitted, *in* those resolutions which the previous action of the church would not suggest, or to which that action would not give rise if the principles before adopted were properly developed. Indeed, so far as appears, it was not made a ground of objection to these resolutions that they did not fairly coincide with the previous positions taken by the Assembly on the subject. In neither of the protests recorded against the action of the Assembly* is it alleged that there was any departure from the previous action of the Presbyterian church, or that the principles before laid down had not been fairly carried out in the paper adopted by the Assembly. The protests are placed wholly on different grounds;—one stating two reasons for protesting, to wit: first, "because they, the protestants, think it inexpedient that the General Assembly should take any action whatever on the subject of slavery,—the General Assembly having at its last session expressed such an opinion as the subject merited; and, in the next place, because they do not believe that slavery, as existing in the Southern States, is forbidden by the laws of God, and the principles of the gospel of Jesus Christ, as revealed in his Holy Word;"—the other stating that the paper adopted by the Assembly, in the opinion of the protestant, "teaches that in every case *some degree of moral turpitude* attaches to every one who holds a slave; and that he ought to be regarded and treated as a subject of discipline, to be instructed, counselled, and exhorted as a delinquent." In neither case is exception taken because the action of the Assembly was supposed to be contrary to any of the judgments of the church before expressed.

(*d*) These resolutions of the Assembly, like all that went before, speak of slavery as an evil, and look to its final and complete extinction as the object to be contemplated and aimed at. They are

---

* There were two protests, one signed by five members of the Assembly, the other by only one.

in the line of the acts of 1818, and, like these acts, aim at the entire abolition of slavery, and in no respect place slavery on the same level with the relation of husband and wife, parent and child, guardian and ward. Thus, the resolutions of the Assembly say, "The system of slavery, as it exists in these United States, viewed either in the laws of the several States which sanction it, or in its actual operation and results in society, is INTRINSICALLY *an unrighteous and oppressive system*, and is opposed to the prescriptions of the law of God, to the spirit and precepts of the gospel, and to the best interests of humanity." Thus, they say, "We cannot withhold the expression of our deep regret that slavery should be *continued and countenanced by any of the members of our churches*, and we do earnestly expect both them, and the churches among whom it exists, *to use all means in their power* TO PUT IT AWAY FROM THEM." And, supposing that this may be a proper subject of discipline, they add, "As a court of our Lord Jesus Christ, we possess no legislative authority; and as the General Assembly of the Presbyterian church, we possess no judiciary authority. We must, therefore, leave this matter with the sessions, and presbyteries, and synods,—the judicatories to whom pertains the right of judgment,—to act *in the administration of discipline* as they may judge to be their duty, constitutionally subject to the Assembly only in the way of general review and control."

It is manifest from this that the Assembly regarded the fact of slave-holding as furnishing *primâ facie* a proper ground of discipline; and the whole spirit of the resolutions goes to show that if it was *not*, in any case, a proper subject of discipline, it was to be *proved* in that particular case not to be, and not to be *assumed* that it was not. Resolutions like these could never have been proposed or adopted in reference to the relations of husband and wife, parent and child, guardian and ward; and it is clear that between those relations and the relations of slavery the Assembly saw no resemblance. In the estimation of the Assembly the relations of slavery were not to be perpetuated as desirable in society, and as consistent with the spirit of the gospel, but as at war with both, and as '*intrinsically unrighteous and oppressive*' in all its bearings.

In 1849 the sentiments of the Assembly were again expressed in a manner not less decisive. After referring the subject to a committee, and after a full consideration of the subject, the Assembly adopted a series of resolutions, the import of which will be seen by the following extracts:—

"1. Resolved, That we reaffirm the sentiments expressed by the Assembly of 1815, and especially in the following quotations:—

"'The General Assembly have repeatedly declared their cordial approbation of those principles of civil liberty which seem to be recognised by the Federal and State Governments in the United States. They have expressed their regret that the slavery of the Africans and of their descendants still continues in so many places, and even among those within the pale of the church, and have urged the presbyteries under their care to adopt such measures as will secure, at least to the rising generation of slaves within the bounds of the church, a religious education, that they may be prepared for the exercise and enjoyment of liberty, when God in his providence may open a door for their emancipation.'

"2. Resolved, That this General Assembly reaffirm the opinions expressed by the General Assembly of 1818.

"3. Resolved, That we reaffirm the 'Declaration of the General Assembly on the subject of slavery,' made in the year 1846.

"The following principles are clearly stated in the documents above referred to and quoted:—

"1. That civil liberty is the right of man, as a rational and moral being.

"2. That the institution of slavery, in the language of a former Assembly, 'is intrinsically an unrighteous and oppressive system,' and injurious to the highest and best interests of all concerned in it.

"3. That it is 'the duty of all Christians who enjoy the light of the present day,' 'to use their honest, earnest, and unwearied endeavours' 'as speedily as possible to efface this blot on our holy religion, and to obtain the complete abolition of slavery throughout Christendom, and, if possible, throughout the world.' This General Assembly do most solemnly exhort all under our care to perform this duty, and to be ever ready to make all necessary sacrifices in order to effect a consummation so much to be desired."

In reference to the action of the Assembly here referred to, it may be observed that there is no retrocession from any of the views which former Assemblies had expressed on the subject; that all that former Assemblies had affirmed in regard to the evils of the system are again reaffirmed and readopted as expressing the sentiments of the church; and that the same ultimate object is still contemplated,—*the entire abolition of slavery*. Thus, after stating, in the language of a former Assembly, that it is "the duty of all Christians who enjoy the light of the present day, to use their honest, earnest, and unwearied endeavours as speedily as possible to efface this blot on our holy religion, and to obtain the complete abolition of slavery throughout Christendom, and, if possible, throughout the world," the Assembly adds, "*The General Assembly do most solemnly exhort all under our care* TO PERFORM THIS DUTY, *and be ever ready to make all necessary sacrifices to effect* A CONSUMMATION SO MUCH TO BE DESIRED." The sentiments and aims here expressed are in the line of all the measures adopted by the church in former years. The system is regarded and treated as evil. The end contemplated is its abolition. The duty of the church, as expressed, lies in that direction, and can only terminate on that. There are no such expressions in regard to the system as there would be in reference to the relation between husband and wife, parent and child, guardian and ward. There is no intimation that it is understood to be a 'patriarchal' institution, that it has the sanction of the Bible, or that it is intended to be perpetual in the church. It is evident that there is but one thing that would be a proper carrying out of the views of the Assembly, and that is, the entire removal of slavery from the church,—its entire abolition in the world.

In the year 1850, the General Assembly, at Detroit, adopted still more decided resolutions on the subject of slavery. After a very full discussion the following preamble and resolutions were adopted:—

"That, after a careful and thorough examination of the whole subject, they have been brought to the conclusion, that, in consideration of the previous action of the Assembly, had at different times for a series of years, and what they believe to be its present sentiments and the expectation of the churches in its connection, the cause of *truth* and *righteousness*, of *peace* and *unity*, will be best subserved by the adoption of the following resolutions :—

"We exceedingly deplore the working of the whole system of slavery as it exists in our country and is interwoven with the political institutions of the slave-holding States, as fraught with many and great evils to the civil, political, and moral interests of those regions where it exists.

"The holding of our fellow-men in the condition of slavery, except in those cases where it is unavoidable, by the laws of the State, the obligations of guardianship, or the demands of humanity, is an offence in the proper import of that term, as used in the Book of Discipline, chap. i. sec. 3, and should be regarded and treated in the same manner as other offences.

"The sessions and presbyteries are, by the Constitution of our church, the courts of primary jurisdiction for the trial of offences.

"That, after this declaration of sentiment, the whole subject of slavery, as it exists in the church, be referred to the sessions and presbyteries, to take such action thereon as in their judgment the laws of Christianity require."

In reference to these resolutions it may be remarked,—

(*a*) That the sentiments of the Assembly, as expressed 'for a series of years,' are adopted as expressing 'the present sentiments' of the church, and as laying the foundation for what was supposed to be demanded as additional action by the church.

(*b*) That the whole system was referred to as an evil to be deplored.

(*c*) But especially a new position was assumed,—a new point was advanced,—in the line indeed of all the previous decisions of the Assembly, and the consistent development of all the former views expressed:—that the holding of men in slavery, except in certain specified cases, is an '*offence*' in the proper and technical sense of the term; that is, is an act subjecting the offender to *discipline*,—an 'offence' to be treated as all other 'offences' are which are regarded as against the word of God.

The exceptional cases referred to are three in number:—(1) When by the laws of the state it is impossible to emancipate slaves; (2) when they are held merely under the obligation and relations of 'guardianship;'. and (3) when the circumstances are such that the laws of 'humanity'—that is, in reference to the best interests of the slave—would forbid emancipation. In every case of slave-holding, therefore, it is supposed that the holder of the slave should be able to show that in that particular case it is proper that the slave should *not* be emancipated, or that it is an impracticable thing to do it. This is the same as to say that a case of ordinary slave-holding—or the holding of a fellow-man *as* a slave—*is* supposed to constitute an 'offence;' and that an obligation rests on the holder of a slave, in any case, to show that *his* act in holding him can be referred to one of those three specified reasons. If this cannot be done, he is presumed to be guilty of an '*offence;*' that is, of an act which subjects him to the proper discipline of the church. In other words, the holding of a slave is *presumed* to be of that class of actions which properly subjects a man to the discipline of the church; not of that class—as the relation of husband and wife, or parent and child—which implies no *primâ facie* presumption against the person who sustains the relation.

It is very manifest that the exceptional cases referred to would comprehend but a small proportion of the owners of slaves in this country. There are undoubtedly such cases; and it is to be presumed that a larger *proportion* of such cases would be found among the members of the church who are slave-holders than could be found in any other class of persons. But still it is to be presumed that but a small part of those who are slave-holders in the church would claim that their cases came under these exceptions, or would allege that they held slaves, as such, on principles different from those which actuate other men sustaining this relation; and especially it is to be presumed that they who allege that the relation is a 'patriarchal' one, and that it is on the same basis as that of husband and wife and parent and child,—a relation recognised in the Bible as proper and permanent,—would not urge that, in this respect, they hold their slaves on different principles from those which influenced others. They *might* perhaps allege that it is better for the slave in the present circumstances to be in this condition than to be free; that he is incapable of taking care of himself; or that the general condition of the African race has been improved by being removed from a land of Pagan darkness to a land of Christian light, even though they *are* slaves. These would be different, and some of them certainly very questionable, positions; but still only a small portion of slave-holders in the church, or out of it, it is presumed, would undertake to show that the reason why they are slave-holders is to be referred to either of the three specifications in the resolutions of the Assembly at Detroit. They would *not* allege that they became originally or continue to be slave-holders because it is 'unavoidable by the laws of the State;' for the cases are rare in which men cannot find *some* way of emancipating their slaves if they choose, since such acts of emancipation *do* occur where the 'laws of the State' are most stringent on the subject of emancipation. They would not allege that they became or continue to be slave-holders under the obligations and relations of 'guardianship;' for it is not common that the slave is *so* held as to be in any sense in that relation. And though there are cases where, against a man's own will, slaves are intrusted to him for his children or for others, yet no one can be *bound* to assume the relation or to hold slaves even in trust for others; and such cases are, in fact, too few almost to be taken into the estimate when considering the subject of slavery. They could not, in most cases, allege that they were held merely or mainly from 'the demands of humanity;' for that would not be true. There may indeed be such cases. An aged, infirm, worn-out slave *may* be thus held. It would be cruel to allow him to be sold; it would be adding injustice to all the former wrongs done him to turn him off when his days have been spent in toiling for another and all his earnings have gone for the support of another,—that then, when from age, or sickness, or exhaustion of his strength, he is unable to labour more, he should be left to be a burden upon a town, or abandoned to die of want. Every consideration of humanity demands that the master who has availed himself of the unrequited toil of such a man should not cast him off in his old age. But *such* cases are few. Such a reason would *rarely* be alleged for holding a slave. The mass of slave-holders, even in the church, do *not* hold slaves for any such purpose. They do not *buy* them with such views; they do not uphold the system on this plea. They hold slaves, as other men do, to avail themselves of their service; they hold them, subject to the same conditions by which they are held by others; they hold them under the same system of laws; they hold them as others do, when they would be liable to be disposed of *as property*, in the same way as other property. And, even if it should be alleged that it is more 'humane' to retain them in this condition than it would be to emancipate them, —a point, however, which should not be *assumed* to be true,—still, this is *not* the reason why they are held. This was not the reason why they came into possession of them. This would not be the reason why, if some perfectly practicable plan were proposed for their emancipation, they would not embrace it. This is not the reason assigned for continuing the relation, when it is alleged that the institution is 'patriarchal,' and that it is represented in the Scriptures as on the same basis as that of parent and child and husband and wife. It is, indeed, more '*humane*' to sustain the relation of a husband than it would be to drive a wife from one's dwelling, or to compel her by ill-treatment to apply for a divorce; it is more '*humane*' for a father to treat his children in the manner that becomes that relation than it would be to compel them by harsh usage to fly from his dwelling and go forth unaided and friendless into the world; but still it may be presumed that *this* is not the reason which operates on the minds of most husbands and fathers in continuing those relations.

It follows from these views that the great body of those who sustain the relation of slave-holders in the church are, according to the resolutions of the Assembly at Detroit, in such a condition as to make them liable to the charge of being guilty of 'an offence in the proper import of this term;' that is, in such a condition as to make them liable to discipline in the same way as in the case of any other 'offence' known to the Constitution of the Presbyterian church. This, I think, is undeniably the fair construction of that act; and for this opinion the Assembly must be regarded as responsible. It is indeed added, and with propriety, that the "sessions and presbyteries are, by the Constitution of the church, the courts of primary jurisdiction for the trial of offences;" but it is presumed that they *will* take "such *action* on the subject as the laws of Christianity require."

In 1851 the subject of slavery again occupied the

attention of the Assembly, when, after a full discussion, the following minute was adopted:—

"The Assembly have reason to be thankful to divine Providence for the wisdom and prudence vouchsafed to the last Assembly, in coming to conclusions on this vexed question which have so generally met with the acquiescence of the church at this crisis; and that it seems obviously our privilege and duty, at the present session, to leave the whole subject as it was placed by that action, and to devote our time to other subjects which demand attention; always praying that God will hasten on the day of universal freedom throughout our land and the world."

Of this resolution it is only necessary to remark that it shows that the subject occupied the attention of the Assembly, and that there was a full concurrence in the principles before established, indicating what were the policy and the aims of the church on the subject.

In 1853 the subject was again discussed, and an important measure adopted, showing the deep interest which the church feels in the subject, and an earnest desire to remove the evil.

This paper is as follows:—

"The committee, to whom was referred the subject of slavery, respectfully report, that twelve memorials touching this grave matter, from various synods and presbyteries, have been put into their hands. Of these, eleven are from the *North*, praying the Assembly for further action, and asking for precise information in regard to the extent of the practice of slave-holding in our body, and in regard also to certain alleged aggravations of it, in the unchristian and cruel treatment of slaves. One is from the *South*, complaining of unkindness and injustice on the part of many Northern brethren in charging upon the memorialists practices of which they are not guilty, and in attributing to them motives which they utterly disclaim and abominate; protesting also against the continued agitation of this subject, as tending more to rivet than to loose the chains of the slave, and seriously to embarrass them in their gospel work.

"Your committee, after much serious and prayerful consideration of this whole subject in all its complicated and perplexing relations, and with a solemn sense of responsibility to God and to his church, are of one mind in recommending to the Assembly the following action:—

"1. That this body reaffirm the doctrine of the 2d resolution adopted by the Assembly in its action at Detroit in 1850.

"2. That we do earnestly exhort and beseech all those who are happily free from any personal connection with the institution of slavery, to exercise patience and forbearance toward their brethren less favoured in this respect than themselves, remembering the embarrassments of their position; and to cherish for them that fraternal confidence and love which they the more need in consequence of the peculiar trials by which they are surrounded.

"3. To correct misapprehensions which may exist in many Northern minds, and allay causeless irritation, by having the real facts in relation to this subject spread before the whole church, it is recommended earnestly to request the presbyteries in each of the slave-holding States to take such measures as may seem to them most expedient and proper, for laying before the next Assembly, in its sessions at Philadelphia, distinct and full statements touching the following points:—

"(1) The number of slave-holders in connection with the churches under their jurisdiction, and the number of slaves held by them.

"(2) The extent to which slaves are held by an unavoidable necessity 'imposed by the laws of the States, the obligations of guardianship, and the demands of humanity.'

"(3) Whether a practical regard, such as the word of God requires, is evinced by the Southern churches for the sacredness of the conjugal and parental relations as they exist among slaves; whether baptism is duly administered to the children of slaves professing Christianity; whether slaves are admitted to equal privileges and powers in the church courts; and, in general, to what extent and in what manner provision is made for the religious well-being of the enslaved."

Of this important paper, adopted by a vote of eighty-four to thirty-nine, the following remarks may be made:—

(*a*) It was clearly within the proper province of the Assembly to propound the inquiries suggested in the paper. No one, it would seem, could properly object to an effort to obtain *information* on any subject pertaining to the state of religion in the church, or to any thing that *affected* religion, from those best qualified to give it, especially when the information sought was to be communicated or not as those most directly interested should deem best. No compulsory measures were instituted or suggested for securing the information; no agents or spies were to be employed; no one was to be questioned; no one was to be subjected to a penalty if he did *not* choose to give the information. Assuredly it would not be improper to endeavour to obtain correct information on *this* subject when the Assembly seeks annually to obtain information by statistical tables, and by written narratives, and by oral reports, of the numbers that are admitted to the church, the numbers that are baptized, the amount of money contributed to benevolent purposes, the manner in which the Sabbath is observed, and the prevalence of any form of immorality in a community where a church is located. If gambling is common, if profaneness abounds, if there are any causes tending to infidelity, if the Sabbath is profaned, if there is a prevalence of licentiousness or intemperance, if there are places where the gospel is not preached, if there are children who have not the advantage of Sabbath-school instruction, the General Assembly feels itself fully competent to seek *information,* from all reliable sources, on these subjects, and to spread that information before the world, and to make the facts ascertained the basis of its own action in promoting the interests of sound morals and religion; and, provided the inquiries are pursued without any inquisitorial prying into the affairs of men, no one feels that the Assembly has transcended its proper bounds. Assuredly, then, on a subject so deeply affecting the interests of religion, and on which there were so many grounds of presumption that the interests of religion would be affected by it, and on which there were so many floating and indefinite rumours in the community, it was proper for the Assembly to seek to obtain exact and reliable information from those best qualified to give it, as the basis of its own future action.

(*b*) The resolutions were entirely *kind* in their nature and their avowed design. They were adopted from no 'inquisitorial' or 'meddling' spirit; from no purpose to give trouble to the Southern churches or to cast suspicion or opprobrium on them. It is but just to those who framed and those who adopted the resolutions, to suppose that the reason stated for their adoption was the true one, unless there is some clear proof to the contrary. That reason is as follows:—"*To correct misapprehensions which may exist in many Northern minds, and allay causeless irritation*, by having the real facts in relation to this subject spread before the whole church." No one can deny that, if this were the real motive for adopting the resolutions, it was in a spirit of entire kindness toward the Southern churches, and with a desire to allay feelings in the North which were caused by a misapprehension of the true state of the case. It was and is constantly alleged, by Southern Christians, that the real facts in regard to slavery are not understood at the North; that the evils are overstated; that there are efforts made for the good of the slaves which are not understood and appreciated by the North; that there are difficulties in the way of emancipation which those who dwell at the North cannot understand; that more is done for the slaves than is commonly supposed; and that if Northern men were themselves in the midst of these scenes they would judge differently from what they do; and the design of these resolutions *seems* to have been to bring out before the world, in an authentic form, precisely the facts which authorize these statements, that the North, as far as possible, *might be* in a condition to form a just estimate on the subject, and that the irritations which had been produced by a want of the information which Southern members of the churches alleged to be in their possession, might be allayed.

(*c*) The resolutions now under consideration gave to the Southern members of the churches an opportunity under this invitation—for it was no more—

to disabuse the public mind at the North, and to bring before the world an authentic statement of the real facts in the case. Of the twelve 'memorials' on which the action of the Assembly was based, one was from the South. That one complained "of unkindness and injustice on the part of many Northern brethren in charging upon the memorialists practices of which they are not guilty, and in attributing to them motives which they utterly disclaim and abominate;" and the resolutions adopted by the Assembly furnished the memorialists themselves, and all others, in their circumstances, with the very best opportunity which could be desired to disabuse themselves on the subject and to state what *were* the real facts in the case. When men complain of wrong done them, of the imputation of improper motives, of injustice in ascribing to them feelings of which they are not conscious, it *seems* to be an act of kindness simply to *ask* them what *are* the facts in the case, and what *are* their real views on a subject in which they are so much interested and where they have so ample means of information. Assuredly there can be no unkindness on the part of men who are *charged* with being in the wrong if they *ask* to be put right, and if they have been accused of judging erroneously, that they seek to obtain the means by which they may be enabled to judge correctly.

(*d*) Moreover, this was a case in which there was no obligation, expressed or implied, to return any answers whatever. It was clearly constitutional and proper to propound these questions; and it was as clearly constitutional and proper *not* to answer them, unless the ministers and members of the Southern churches should suppose that it was proper, and that the interests of brotherhood, religion, and humanity, would be promoted by it. Whatever might be thought in regard to the subject on the score of *courtesy*, when, in such circumstances, and for such purposes, questions are seriously proposed by Christian brethren and they are wholly disregarded, it is clear that no *right* was violated, and that no such wrong was done as to justify any further notice of it by the Assembly. Accordingly, when it appeared in the meeting of the Assembly in 1854 that the great body of the Southern churches had not even *noticed* in any way the resolutions of the Assembly proposing these inquiries, and that, in the three or four instances in which they had been noticed, the returns made to the Assembly were not even in the respectful form of *written* communications, but in the presentation of *newspapers* containing printed resolutions of presbyteries at the South, alike complaining of the action of the Assembly and refusing to give any information on the subject, it was obviously proper that the Assembly should press the subject no further, and Christian courtesy and the desire to avoid any additional cause of irritation demanded that no notice should be taken of the neglect of the Southern churches to adopt the mode proposed of disabusing themselves, and setting themselves right before the world in the very case where they alleged that they had reason to "complain of unkindness and injustice on the part of Northern brethren, in charging upon them practices of which they are not guilty, and in attributing to them motives which they utterly disclaim and abominate." Accordingly, the Assembly properly dropped the subject, and did nothing to press inquiries which the Southern churches seemed to regard as so improper and so discourteous. If I am under a misapprehension in regard to another, and am in danger unintentionally of doing him injustice, and am actually charged with doing him injustice, and if I simply *ask* the means of judging correctly in the case, and he does not choose to give me the information, my sense of the obligations of Christian courtesy would not allow me to press the subject further, or even to reproach him for a neglect of what would seem to be so just to himself and so kind to me.

(*e*) This action of the Assembly showed what are the established views of the Presbyterian church on the subject of slavery. It was in the line of all former acts and decisions. The action of the Assembly at Detroit in 1850 is solemnly 'reaffirmed.' Slavery, according to that action, is regarded as an 'offence,' and to be treated as such. It is contemplated as a relation wholly different from that of husband and wife, parent and child, guardian and ward. It is evidently, according to these resolutions, a system not to be perpetuated but removed; it is assumed that a man who sustains this relation is not, *primâ facie*, in good standing in the church; but that, if he sustains that relation, his good standing *is to be made out* by showing that he holds his slaves by "an unavoidable necessity imposed by the laws of the States, the obligations of guardianship, and the demands of humanity."

There remains but one other act of the General Assembly to be noticed as indicating the position of the New-school Presbyterian church on the subject of slavery. The most solemn testimony had been repeatedly borne against the system,—testimony so explicit and so often repeated that it would seem that it would avail nothing if it were reiterated; the subject had been discussed in all its bearings and relations, and with a freedom with which it had never been approached in any other body in our country; the Assembly had repeatedly, and in the most solemn manner, declared that the end contemplated was "the entire abolition of slavery;" the churches where it prevails had been exhorted to use every practicable measure to detach themselves wholly from the system; it had been declared by two Assemblies to be an *offence* in the proper and technical sense of the term,—in the sense that the member of the church who was a slaveholder was liable to *discipline* in the same way as any other offender, unless he could show that the circumstances in which he held slaves were such as to make it "unavoidable by the laws of the State, the obligations of guardianship, or the demands of humanity;" and a solemn and earnest request, which the result showed was entirely unheeded, had been sent to the churches where slavery prevails, to ascertain and report the exact *facts* in the case, that they might thus "correct misapprehensions and allay causeless irritation."

What could be done next? What power had the church to move further? Had the limit of its power been reached? Were the means of reaching and removing the evil exhausted? Was there no step which could still be taken? Or must the church sit

down now in hopeless despair as to the probability that the evil would ever be removed?

To meet and answer these questions, the subject, in 1855, was referred to a committee, at the meeting of the Assembly in St. Louis, to report to the next Assembly on the constitutional powers of the Assembly on the subject. The resolution appointing the committee, as finally adopted, is in the following words:—"That the General Assembly hereby reaffirm the testimony of past Assemblies in regard to the sinfulness of the system of slavery as it generally exists in these United States, and express their deep regret at the intemperateness of word and action which has too often characterized the spirit of those who have conscientiously aimed at its overthrow; and that they urge upon their churches earnest efforts, by all Christian and constitutional modes, to remove the evil from the midst of us.

"That a committee be appointed to report to the next Assembly on the constitutional power of the Assembly over the subject of slave-holding in our churches; and that we recommend that this evil be removed from our church as soon as it can be done in a Christian and constitutional manner." (Minutes of the Assembly for 1855, pp. 34–36.)

Of these resolutions it may be remarked,—

(*a*) That there is no retrocession on the subject of slavery. All the solemn testimonies of former Assemblies are reaffirmed in regard to the evil of the system.

(*b*) It is a renewed testimony against the 'SINFULNESS' of the system of slavery. It is regarded as *sinful*, and so treated. It is in no sense spoken of as

a proper or desirable relation, or as a system which is to be perpetuated in the church.

(*c*) The same great object is aimed at which has marked *all* the acts of the General Assembly of the Presbyterian church from 1787:—*the entire and total abolition of slavery.* Thus, they urge upon the churches "earnest efforts, by all Christian and constitutional modes, TO REMOVE THE EVIL FROM THE MIDST OF US;" and thus they "recommend *that this evil be* REMOVED *from our church as soon as it can be done in a Christian and constitutional manner.*" The system is *never* contemplated in the Presbyterian church as one that is to be perpetuated, or that is on the same level as the relation of parent and child, guardian and ward. It is an *evil;* it is a *sinful* system; it is a system that is to be wholly '*removed*' as soon as it can be done.

The committee appointed in 1855 reported the present year the following paper, which was adopted by the Assembly:—

"The Committee appointed by the last General Assembly 'to report to the next Assembly on the constitutional power of the Assembly over the subject of slave-holding in our churches,' respectfully submit the following report:—

"It should be observed, at the outset, that the Committee are instructed to report on but a single point,—that of 'power.' The question before them is not what it may be wise for the Assembly to do; not what, in a particular case, or in general, —authority being presupposed,—would be for edification; but what is the *power* of the Assembly in the matter of slave-holding. This is a question which can be determined only by reference to our Form of Government. The 'power' on which we are to report is fitly designated as 'constitutional.' We are a constitutional body. No judicatory of our church has any legitimate functions, save those which, either expressly or by clear implication, the Constitution confers. Emphatically should this be said of our highest judicatory, in view of the tendency of human nature, in ecclesiastical connections, to a grasping and tyrannous centralism. The one-man power at Rome is hardly more abhorrent to the genius of Presbyterianism than would be a many-headed Papacy under the name and form of a General Assembly. It should be remembered, also, that as a visible church, or particular denomination, our Constitution is the sole bond of our union. We are united, externally and formally, only as that unites us. That, of course, must measure and limit the responsibility for each other which grows out of our union. No one part of our body can be held answerable for the evils in another, which, by the terms of our confederation, it has no power to reach.

"The Committee would further remark that they do not feel themselves called on to present their views of the moral character of slavery, or to re-argue the question whether slaveholding is, in any case, a disciplinable offence. They do not suppose that they were appointed with reference to that question. It was thoroughly discussed in the Assembly of 1850, and the conclusion reached, 'that the holding of our fellowmen in the condition of slavery, except in those cases where it is unavoidable by the laws of the State, the obligations of guardianship, or the demands of humanity, is an offence in the proper import of that term, as used in the Book of Discipline, chapter 1, section 3, and should be regarded and treated in the same manner as other offences.' This opinion has been reaffirmed, either expressly or virtually, by nearly every succeeding Assembly, including the last. Nor do the Committee anticipate that any considerable portion of the present Assembly will either stand in doubt concerning it, or incline in the least to a retrograde course. The doctrine set forth at Detroit—set forth simply as a doctrine, and not as a law or judicial decision—is yet, they judge, the settled view of our church. Taking this for granted, their sole concern is with the relation of the Assembly to the matter. To determine this point, we have only to ascertain what are the constitutional powers of that body in respect to disciplinable offences generally.

"Its functions, in this regard, we judge, are of two kinds,—*advisory* and *authoritative;* and between these there should be careful discrimination. The *advisory* function of the Assembly is of very wide scope. According to the Form of Government, chapter 12, section 5, they have the power of 'reproving, warning, or bearing testimony against error in doctrine or immorality in practice in any church, presbytery, or synod,' and 'of recommending reformation of manners through all the churches under their care.' This function of reproof may be exercised in reference to any evil grave enough to call for it. Nor is it an unimportant function. The testimony of such a body as the General Assembly, especially if unanimously given, must needs have great weight. It has, indeed, only a *moral* influence. It is not authoritative. It binds no other body; not even a succeeding Assembly. It binds no individual; yet cases are not unfrequent in which a moral influence of this sort, if not the only one that could be employed, is the most efficacious. It has greater power over the conscience, often, than the most stringent exercise of bare authority.

"As it respects the *authoritative* function of the Assembly, or its power of discipline, that, we judge, can only be exercised in the forms and methods marked out in the Constitution. It is by no means coextensive with its testifying power. As counsel or testimony has only a moral force, the manner in which it shall be put forth is wisely left to the discretion of the Assembly. Not so with discipline. Concerning, as it does, the dearest rights and interests, it is of the highest importance that the mode of its exercise should be particularly prescribed. So we find it in our Form of Government.

Every step is distinctly set forth, and the greatest care taken to guard all concerned against mistake and abuse. Nor is any exception made as to any particular class of offences. If slave-holding is in any case to be dealt with as a disciplinable matter, it must be in some one of the ways explicitly authorized in the Constitution.

"The methods in which the *authoritative* action of the Assembly may be invoked, as appears from the seventh chapter of the Book of Discipline, are four:—By *reference*, by *appeal*, by *complaint*, and—to state that last which, in the Book of Discipline, comes first—by *general review and control.* The three processes first named do not, of course, originate in the Assembly. Their inception is in a lower judicatory. In one or another of them, it is presumed, most of the matters which call for disciplinary action on the part of the highest judicatory will, in due time, come before it. There is, however, a possibility of neglect in this regard, and, for such a contingency, our Constitution—framed with a wisdom best appreciated by those who have most thoroughly studied it—has made a specific provision. This provision is found in the section on 'General Review and Control.' See Book of Discipline, chapter 7, section 1.

"Under this section, there are two methods in which any disciplinable offence—and slave-holding, of course, when it assumes that character—may be reached authoritatively by the Assembly. (1) It may appear from the records of a synod, as submitted for inspection, that there has been some wrong-doing or culpable omission in the matter. A case may have been incorrectly decided, or refused a hearing. Or it may be obvious that the records of some presbytery have not, according to the 2d and 3d articles of this section, been properly disposed of. Or it may appear that the duty enjoined in the 6th article—that of citing a lower judicatory in a given contingency—has been entirely neglected. In cases of this sort, there may be 'animadversion or censure,' or, according to article 3, the synod 'may be required to review and correct its proceedings.' (2) 'Any important delinquency, or grossly unconstitutional proceedings,' not apparent from the records, may yet be charged against a synod 'by common fame.' It may be reported, for example, that, through some neglect of the synod, 'heretical opinions or corrupt practices' are 'allowed to gain ground,' or that 'offenders of a very gross character' are 'suffered to escape.' See articles 5 and 6 of this same section. In such case, provided the rumour is of the character specified in the Book of Discipline, chapter 3, section 5,—for a process against a synod should certainly not be commenced on slighter grounds than against an individual,—the Assembly 'is to cite the judicatory alleged to have offended, to appear at a specified time and place, and to show what it has done, or failed to do, in the case in question; after which the judicatory thus issuing the citation shall remit the whole matter to the delinquent judicatory, with a direction to take it up, and dispose of it in a constitutional manner, or stay all further proceedings in the case, as circumstances may require.' See Book of Discipline, chapter 7, section 1, article 6.

"In view of the aforenamed and other provisions of our Form of Government, touching the authority of the Assembly, two things are to be carefully noted.

"1. It has no power to *commence* a process of discipline with an individual offender. That, by a just and wise arrangement, belongs to the session in the case of a layman, to the presbytery in the case of a minister. The disciplinary function of the Assembly, as to individuals, is simply appellate and revisionary. It is not the court of first, but of last, resort.

"2. In the way of 'general review and control,' it can reach *directly* only the judicatory next below; that is, the synod. See Book of Discipline, chapter 7, section 1, article 6. Indirectly, indeed, the doings of other bodies may be involved. A session may grossly neglect discipline, for example, and the recorded indication, or the common fame thereof, may not be properly heeded by the presbytery. The fruit of this heedlessness, or the evidence of it in the presbyterial records, may call forth no appropriate action on the part of the synod; and this may be brought, by the synodical records, or by general rumour, to the knowledge of the Assembly. On the ground of either the record or the rumour, the Assembly may cite the synod before them. Thus, *mediately*, may even a session be reached, but not directly.

"Such are the metes and bounds which our Form of Government has prescribed, and which the Assembly may not overpass. It is quite possible that, in connection with them, offenders of various sorts may sometimes escape. To a human administration, of however divine a system, imperfection always pertains. Our Book of Discipline, indeed, (chapter 3, section 3,) distinctly recognises a class of cases in which, 'however grievous it may be to the pious to see an unworthy member in the church, it is proper to wait until God, in his righteous providence, shall give further light.' Waiting may be rendered necessary by a lack of fidelity on the part of the lower judicatories, as well as by a lack of evidence. We speak of it, of course, not as an actual, but only as a supposable, case. And it may seem to some a great evil that the General Assembly is not invested with larger powers. Yet it would be a greater evil to allow any departure from the carefully-devised processes of discipline set forth in the Constitution. To permit the Assembly to adopt, at its pleasure, new processes—to suit its own powers to real or fancied exigencies—would not only invest it with legislative functions, but would virtually annul the Constitution, and transform the highest judicatory of the church into an overshadowing ecclesiastical despotism.

"It has, indeed, been urged—though we see not with what reason—that the advisory function of the Assembly, or its power of bearing testimony, implies the authority necessary to enforce that testimony. Is there, then, no just and salutary distinction between persuasion and compulsion? Must the two be ever conjoined? Are there no cases in which a simple moral power may, in the nature of things, be most potent? Must the Assembly utter no counsels which are not to be interpreted as mandatory and coercive? If they may enforce all their counsels, how are they to do it? By processes which they themselves devise?—extra-constitutional processes? Or are they to be held to the provisions of the Book of Discipline? They have, it is true, the right, according to the Form of Government, chapter 12, section 5, of 'attempting,' as well as 'recommending, reformation of manners.' But the attempt must be made, if discipline is to be involved, only in the method prescribed in the Constitution. To all desirable ends, the Committee believe that method will be found adequate, especially as connected with that testifying and reproving function so often exercised in time past, and which, by a body like the Assembly, can never be wisely exercised but with salutary results."

In reference to this paper the following remarks may be made:—

(*a*) The Assembly adopted, as its own, the action of the Assembly at Detroit, which declared that "the holding of our fellow-men in the condition of slavery, except in those cases where it is unavoidable by the laws of the State, the obligations of guardianship, or the demands of humanity, is an '*offence*' in the proper import of the term;"—thus placing it, in all cases except those specified, among the sins which subject a man to the discipline of the church. This the committee—and the Assembly by adopting their report—say, is "the settled view of the church."

(*b*) There is no retrocession—no returning—'to a retrograde course.' There is no abandonment of any former 'testimony;' no modification of any previous doctrine promulgated by the Assembly on the subject; no intimation that any other ground was to be taken than that which had been taken in all the previous acts of the Assembly. The only inquiry before the committee, and the only point on which the Assembly acted, had reference to the '*power*' of the Assembly, as a constitutional body, in carrying out the views which had been uniformly proclaimed on the subject of slavery.

(*c*) The same great object is manifestly contemplated which had been pursued so long, and which was so distinctly declared in the resolutions of 1818, —the 'total abolition of slavery.' It was with reference to the mode of doing this, and the power of the Assembly to do it, that the committee was appointed. It was not contemplated in that appointment that they should suggest any way by which slavery could be perpetuated, or by which the relation could be made to appear to be in accordance with the principles of the gospel, or to recommend any method by which the conscience of a slave-holder could be relieved while sustaining that relation. The appointment of the committee had one end only; and that end is reconcilable *only* with the view that slave-holding is an evil, and that some 'power' *should be* exercised over those who sustain that relation. What would have been the proper interpretation of an act appointing a committee to inquire into the constitutional power of the Assembly over the relations of parent and child, husband and wife, guardian and ward? What but that *in* these relations there was something so evil, or so dangerous, as to demand the interposition of the authority of the church? What would be the fair interpretation of an act of the Assembly appointing a committee to inquire into the 'constitutional power of the Assembly' in relation to any of its members who might be engaged in selling lottery-tickets, or in prosecuting a business that necessarily led to a violation of the Sabbath, or in relation to those who rent their property for purposes of pollution or gambling? What but that it was supposed that there was something in such a mode of life as to demand the interposition of the Assembly in removing it, as a scandal, from the church? No other interpretation than this can be fairly given to the act of the Assembly in appointing the committee on the subject of slave-holding; no other duty was understood by the majority of the committee to have been assigned them.

(*d*) In accordance with this view, the whole report of the committee is based on the fact that slave-holding *is*, *primâ facie*, a disciplinable 'offence,' and that there is a regular way by which, as such, it may be brought before the Assembly. The committee regarded it as nothing else; and the only real inquiry before them was, how it might be constitutionally reached so as to be removed from the church.

The subject of slavery, therefore, has been more fully discussed in the New-school Presbyterian church in this country than by any other denomination of Christians. No other denomination has had the subject so often before it, or met it so frankly and fearlessly. No denomination has borne so frequent and so decided a testimony against it. None has sought so earnestly and so steadily to remove the evil from its own bounds or from the land. The position of the New-school church on the subject is perfectly defined. No one need mistake it: it would seem that it would be impossible to mistake it. The sentiments of the church on the subject are well known to its own ministers and members: they are proclaimed before the world.

From the review of the successive steps taken by the Presbyterian church, the following results seem to be fully established as indicating the position of the church on the subject:—

1. Slave-holding is regarded as an *evil.* It is a different relation altogether from that of husband and wife, parent and child, guardian and ward. It is held to be contrary to the precepts of the Bible and to the spirit of Christianity. This has been expressed in every variety of way, and without any ambiguity or any wavering. The principles asserted so constantly and so long by the Presbyterian church cannot be carried out under the idea that slavery is *not* an evil, or that it is *not* unlike the relations in life just referred to. There has been no such legislation in regard to them: no such legislation in regard to them would be attempted or tolerated either at the South or the North.

It is sometimes asked whether slavery is to be regarded as a *sin per se,*—or a sin *in itself;* and much learned dust is sometimes thrown in reference to this question, assisting much in the effort to mystify the subject and to escape from the charge of criminality. The General Assembly of the Presbyterian church has not attempted to discuss this abstract matter, as it has not in regard to the sin *per se* of horse-racing or lotteries; and it might be possible to create as much mystery by discussing the question about the abstract nature of sin in reference to those subjects as in reference to slavery. The truth is, that, except for purpose of mystification,—for the purpose of throwing dust in the eyes of another,—for the purpose of escaping from responsibility in a fog,—for the purpose of indulging in sin while the mind is diverted by an abstract question,—and for the purpose of perplexing an adversary,—we never start the question whether any thing is a sin *per se* at all. When, however, a man desires to sell lottery-tickets, nothing is more convenient than to suggest the inquiry whether it is a sin *per se* to make this kind of appeal to chance; when a man is hard pressed by arguments for temperance, and desires to indulge in wine as a beverage, or even in stronger drink, nothing is more convenient for his purpose than to start the question whether it is to be regarded as a sin *per se* to partake of fermented liquors or alcoholic drinks; when a priest or a Levite would *wish* for any cause to pass by a wounded man, nothing can be more convenient than to start the inquiry whether this could be regarded as a sin *per se*. Few would be the clear moral decisions which men would make if they should pause at every step to settle this abstract question; few are the questions of morals, however plain to common minds, which could not be mystified and made very doubtful if this point were to be settled before men should act. As a matter of plain, practical, every-day concern, it is not desirable to put any of these questions in this form; in reference to sound policy and sound action in a community, it is not wise to open any of these matters to the endless logomachies which attend such abstract inquiries.

Two things seem to be all that is needful to be said on the question whether slavery is to be regarded as a sin *per se*.

(*a*) One is, that, if it is meant that there may *possibly* be a case where the relation is not sinful, this *may be so*. This was expressly assumed in the resolutions adopted at Detroit, if slave-holding in any case is "unavoidable by the laws of the State, or by the obligations of guardianship, or by the demands of humanity." That such cases *may* occur there can be no reason to doubt; how frequent they are, is another question altogether. It is to be presumed, however, that they comprise but *few* of all the cases of slave-holding in the land. Few slave-holders defend the fact that they hold men in bondage on these grounds; few advocates of slavery at the North maintain that these cases constitute the general rule and not the exceptions. All those, with very few exceptions, who regard slave-holding in general as sinful, suppose that there *may* be cases where the mere legal relation cannot be regarded as wrong. If a purchase is made at the request of a slave, and with a view to his freedom; if he is held merely *in transitu*, and with the design that he shall be free; if an aged slave in a family is so held in order that he may be provided for, and so held that he might be free if he chose, and that he would not be sold if his *nominal* master should die; or if the young who are inherited as slaves are held with a view to freedom, and under a proper training for freedom, and with suitable security that they shall be free when they reach a certain age or should their legal owner die,—it would seem to be plain that these cases are consistent with the spirit of Christianity, and that a man should not feel that he is guilty before God if he is in these circumstances. But, at the same time, it should be said that it ought to be a matter of devout gratitude to any one to be able to reflect that he is not in that condition himself, and that his mind will be more at ease if, even in *this* sense, he is wholly detached from slavery.

(*b*) But, if it is contemplated that a slave is to be held *as* a slave,—as property; if he is bought and sold for purposes of gain; if his freedom is not contemplated or desired; if no arrangements are made for his emancipation while his owner lives or when he dies; if there is no express and definite training *for* freedom; if the whole system of discipline is such as to fit him for slavery and not for freedom; if the slave is so held that when his master dies he will be subject to the same mode of disposal as any other 'property;' if he is liable to be sold into harder bondage, to be separated from his wife and children, to be consigned to perpetual servitude,—then slave-holding *is* a sin *per se*, and should be dealt with as any other sin is. If such be the aim and the purpose of the slave-holder, then, in reply to the question whether slavery is a 'sin *per se*,' I answer, in the words of another, "It is a sin, as murder is sin, as theft is sin, as injustice is sin. Cases there may be where slave-holders are only *nominally* guilty. The same is true of many acts which, in view of human law, are called murder and theft. A man may be a nominal slave-holder from necessity, and yet be a pious and benevolent man. A murderer in the judgment of man may be acquitted at the bar of God. In both these cases a false judgment exists. There is neither slave-holding nor murder in either case. But when a man kills another from *malice*, it is murder; when a man holds slaves for *gain*, it is injustice and fraud. Here is the true distinction. Any man who holds slaves *for a benevolent end*,—who remunerates their labour, and is only prevented from manumitting them by circumstances which he cannot control,—is involved in *misfortune*, but not in *guilt;* but he who holds slaves for his *own gain*, to increase his wealth, or to promote his selfish ends, is as truly guilty of injustice and fraud as if he were a common thief; and he is all the more guilty, because he robs the slave of rights far more precious than gold. A *single act* of robbery dooms a thief to the State prison; a *system* of robbery is justified and defended, and is no bar to honour and respectability in the world."*

These are, in my apprehension, sound moral principles; nor is it possible for me to see how, if a slave is held for purposes of *gain* and not for a purpose of benevolence, the act can be regarded otherwise than as a 'sin *per se*,'—a sin like all other sins *in itself*,—and that it should be so treated and regarded.

---

* Slavery and the Church, by Smectymnuus, Boston, 1856, p. 8. This is by an Old-school Presbyterian.

2. It is a clear principle in the Presbyterian church, as defined by the successive acts of the church represented in the General Assembly, that slavery is not regarded as a good to be perpetuated, but as an evil to be removed. There is not an act of the church, from the beginning of its history in this country, that can, by any fair interpretation, be adduced to prove that slavery is to be perpetuated, or that it is contemplated as a thing which it is desirable to continue in the world. All the acts of the Assembly from the beginning look in one direction; all contemplate one end:—the total abolition of slavery in the church and in the world. The inquiries which have been started and pursued with so much earnestness now for a period of more than fifty years have not been how it may be perpetuated, but how it may be removed. There has been no legislation with a view to its perpetuity; there has been none so to modify the system that it might thus become a relation desirable to be perpetuated; there has been no direct and exclusive action in regard to the *abuses* of the system. All the acts of the Assembly have been aimed at the thing itself, as a great evil which the best interests of religion made it desirable to have removed as soon as possible. There has been indeed much kindness and forbearance in the spirit of all the acts of the Assembly. There has been much sympathy expressed for the Southern churches who are involved in the misfortunes and disadvantages incident to slavery. There has been no disposition to press matters to an extreme. There has been no disposition to cut even slave-holders off from the

church by summary legislation. There has been a firm and fixed regard to the Constitution of the church. There has been much inquiry and much prayer about the proper way to reach the evil; but there has been an *intention to reach it.* There has been one steady, long-continued, persevering effort to reach it; and, so far as the action of the church has gone, it has been of the same nature as that pursued in relation to intemperance, Sabbath-breaking, profaneness, gambling, lotteries, horse-racing, and licentiousness,—a steady inquiry, not how these evils might be perpetuated in the community, but how they might be removed; an inquiry, not how they might be rendered tolerable by checking abuses, but how they might be removed altogether; an inquiry, not whether it was *desirable* to remove them, but only how it might be done. Emancipation, entire and universal, has been in the line of all the action on the subject of slavery, and would have been accomplished long ago if the often-expressed wishes of the church had been complied with, or if there had been power to reach the evil.

3. It follows from the various acts of the Assembly, as they have now been considered, that a man who is a slave-holder is not *primâ facie* in good standing in the Presbyterian church. It is a case for him to make out; not for him to assume to be true. There may be cases, as has been shown, where a man is not to be regarded as subject to the discipline of the church, or as guilty of an '*offence*,' who sustains the *legal* relation of a slave-holder; but that is a case for him to *make out*. It is true that slave-holding has

existed in the Presbyterian church, as in all other churches in this country, from the beginning; it is true that there has been no formal act of the church declaring that a man who sustains this relation cannot, in any circumstances, be regarded as in good standing in the church; it is true that there have been no formal acts of discipline excluding a man from the church for sustaining this relation; it is true that many have entered the church supposing that the act of slave-holding was no bar to good standing; and it is true that in the General Assembly slave-holding ministers and elders have been admitted to seats without a question being raised as to their regular standing in the church. But all this does not change the essential inference derived from the action of the church on the subject. How *can* a man who is a slave-holder regard himself as occupying precisely the same position in the church as he does who sustains the relation of husband, father, guardian? Against the one relation there has been a long and steady course of action for fifty years, speaking uniformly of the system as "evil; as contrary to the Bible and the spirit of Christianity; as a gross violation of the most precious and sacred rights of human nature; as a paradox in the moral system; as a blot on our holy religion; as a system to be totally removed as speedily as possible." How can a man, if he respects these uniform and reiterated declarations of his own church,—declarations made before he entered it, existing on its records when he entered it, and repeated constantly since he entered it,—how can he regard himself, or suppose that the church regards him, as in perfectly fair and good standing in a church where these are the avowed and settled principles, who holds his fellow-men in a condition where they are exposed to all these evils? Suppose that the same course of legislation had been pursued in regard to lotteries, and a member of the church still persisted in selling lottery-tickets and was tolerated, not because his conduct was approved, but because there was no constitutional power to bring him under any act of discipline; or in regard to the manufacture and sale of ardent spirits, and a member of the church still persevered in manufacturing and selling the poison; or in regard to horse-racing, and a member of the church still persisted in engaging in this species of business; or in regard to the *slave-trade*, and a member of the church still continued to pursue the traffic: would it be proper to assume that such a man was *primâ facie* in good standing in the church, and that, other things being equal, he was to be regarded as precisely in the same condition as the man who sustains the relation of father, husband, or guardian? The Presbyterian church by its acts regards the holding of slaves as an '*offence*,'—that is, an act subjecting a man to the discipline of the church,—unless he can show that, in his case, from peculiar circumstances, it is *not* to be so treated. And, according to the acts of that church, this offence is to be approached and reached as any other 'offence' is; and nothing in the nature of the act, or the relation as such, separates it in the estimate in which it is to be held and in the manner in which it is to be treated, in the recorded judgment of the church, from any other act subjecting a man to discipline.

These, so far as I can understand the acts of the church, are settled principles. This is the position of the Presbyterian church on this subject. These are the ends and aims which have been contemplated now for a period of half a century. The declaration of sentiment has been steady; the aim has been steady. The ultimate avowed object from the beginning has been the 'total abolition of slavery' in the church, and, as far as possible, in the world; the inquiries pursued have been only *how* this end might best be reached. There have been no back-tracks taken; there has been no ambiguity in regard to this as being the ultimate design. If there has been an intermitting of testifying on the subject, it has not been because there has been any change of view or purpose; if the church has seemed to slumber over the subject, it has been because some other important matter claimed more immediate attention, or because it seemed that a mere repetition of former testimonies in regard to the subject would only irritate without promoting the object; if there has been an omission to *act*, it was because it was not apparent what further could be done; if there has been a kind word uttered in behalf of the churches where the evil prevails, it was not to apologize for the evil, but to prevent a severity of judgment and a harshness of expression in regard to those who, by no agency of their own, have been placed in these circumstances; and if there has been a word of severity uttered in regard to abolitionists, it has not been because they were aiming to 'effect the total abolition of slavery,' but because some of them made war on the Bible, on the church, and on the ministry; it has been because they were promoting infidelity at the same time that they were promoting a good cause, or under colour of promoting a good cause,—not because they are the enemies of slavery.

Such a position I regard as a noble position. It has given the New-school Presbyterian church an elevation, in this respect, above the branch of the church from which it has been separated, and above all the other churches in this land. Its position is better determined than that of any other church; the subject has had a more full discussion in that church than in any other. Difficulties have been encountered which are yet to be encountered by every other great denomination of Christians in this land, and which, in the discussion, *may* do to them what it has *not* done to the New-school Presbyterian church,—break them asunder or scatter them in fragments. The positions taken in that church have placed it, in this respect, in a condition that accords with the spirit of the age in regard to slavery; with all the noble sentiments that prevail in the world on the subject, and with all the genuine utterances of humanity. In this respect it is abreast, if not ahead, of the world.

For one, I glory in this position, and deem it an honour to belong to a church where these sentiments have been uttered; these positions taken; and these ends avowed. I would not remain connected with a church—no, not for one hour—if I believed that it was contemplated that slavery was to be a permanent institution in that church; if it was held that the relation is on the same basis as that of husband and wife, parent and child, master and apprentice, guardian and ward; if it was understood that the relation implied nothing against a man's good and regular standing in the church; and if the "complete abolition of slavery throughout Christendom, and, if possible, throughout the world," was not the aim contemplated and steadily pursued by all Christian and constitutional methods. If such were not the aim of the church with which I was connected, I would seek some other connection; or, if I could not find such a connection in a church that would be in general accordance with my views on other matters, I would stand alone, and give utterance to a solitary testimony against this great evil,—"this blot on our holy religion." I would go down, as I intend to now, to the closing scene of my life with the reflection that, though my name might be worth little, it could not be adduced as in any way, or by any fair construction, contributing to the support and perpetuity of this system, or as being connected with a church which contemplated this as among the permanent institutions of the world. *My* death-bed shall never be clouded by any such recollection; and no man after my death shall be able to refer to me as having even once in my life uttered a sentiment in favour of human bondage, or as having contributed even by my silence to its extension and perpetuity in the world.

CHAPTER VI.

THE CONSTITUTIONAL POWER OF THE PRESBYTERIAN CHURCH ON THE SUBJECT OF SLAVERY.

It is a very material inquiry now, whether all has been done by the church that can be done to check the progress of slavery and to remove it from the world; whether the resources of the church are exhausted; whether Christianity at this point is powerless; whether the church, having borne its testimony against the evil, must sit down exhausted and despair of doing any thing further; or whether there is still a work to be accomplished, that shall be in the proper line of the functions of the church, for detaching itself from the evil, and for removing it from our land and from the world. *Must* the church stand where it is, and leave the evil to grow or to correct itself? *Must* it, confessing its own weakness, make it over now to politicians and to worldly men? *Must* it, having made a record of its sentiments on the subject, now fold its arms and look to the providence of God alone to interpose and check the evil?

No man with just views will doubt that there is need of the interposition of divine Providence in removing such an evil as slavery from the world; no man with just views will make any effort to remove the evil without feeling that all success must depend on that God who has power over men's hearts, and who can dispose them to do what is right,—"to unloose the heavy burdens, and to bid the oppressed go free." Still, it is a proper and a fair inquiry whether there is any thing that remains to be done by the church to "efface this blot on our holy religion," and to secure "liberty to all the inhabitants of the land." This inquiry will be pursued first with reference to the New-school Presbyterian church, and then with reference to the church at large.

In reference to the New-school Presbyterian church (and the same remarks would be applicable to some other denominations) there are two points worthy of remark. One relates to the fact that it is a *constitutional* body; the other to the inquiry what can be done under that Constitution, and consistently with it, in reaching and removing the evil.

1. It is a constitutional body; that is, it has principles of doctrine and rules of practice which have been agreed on, and which are to be observed in all its acts of government and discipline. The general *principles* contained, as it is supposed, in the New Testament, have been embodied and arranged for the organization and the government of the church. It is not supposed either that the principles of the Constitution are of higher authority than the Bible; or that there is any thing in the Constitution which cannot be found substantially in the Bible; or that its rules and laws are binding should they contravene the laws of the Bible; or that they bind the conscience as such in the same sense that the laws of the Bible do; or that they cannot be altered if it

should be found necessary in order to make them more conformable to the Bible. The arrangement is *conventional;* and it is *agreed*, by those who become ministers and members of that church, that, while connected with it, they will conform to the specified rules and arrangements in the Form of Government and Discipline. It is an admitted principle with all true Presbyterians that the Constitution must be complied with or altered; that in reference to all evils, and the methods of removing them, the forms specified in the Constitution should be strictly observed, or that they should be, in a proper way, so changed as to meet that form of evil; that a man who is not willing to pursue this course, and who should seek to introduce some form of meeting an evil not known to the Constitution, violates a compact solemnly made when he connected himself with the church. There is a proper course for such a man. It is to seek, in a regular way, to have the Constitution so changed as to meet his views, or, failing in this, quietly to withdraw from the church and seek another connection.

At the same time, it is to be observed that the Constitution of the church MAY BE ALTERED. Venerable as it is, valuable as it is, and wise as it is, it is not to be *assumed* that all wisdom died with the fathers; nor is it to be assumed that they had the gift of inspiration to understand *all* that there is in the Bible, or that comprehensive power which could condense *all* which it contains into a brief constitution. Nor had they the gift of such extraordinary foreknowledge as to be able to anticipate all the contingencies which might occur, or all the phases of error and sin which might at any future time exist in the church and the world. If slave-holding *is* a sin, and *if* the Constitution has not made provision for removing it, it is not to be *assumed* that it is *therefore* to be perpetual in the church, and that it is forever to be protected by the sanction of a constitution. The true way would be to meet it as any *other* evil would be met which had been before misunderstood, or which had not been comprehended in the arrangements made by the framers of the Constitution. It is rather to be assumed that there is *no* evil which is beyond the reach of the church; *no* iniquity which is to be permanently and perpetually tolerated because the fathers who made the Constitution were not sagacious, wise, and foreseeing enough to anticipate its existence, or to embrace it in the provisions which they made for removing evil.

Nor is it to be *assumed*, because the same thing existed when the Constitution was made, and was tolerated then, that THEREFORE it is *always* to be tolerated. This would be to make the framers of the Constitution more keen-sighted and sagacious than any framers of a constitution have ever been, and would be to place them on an eminence in authority which it would be difficult to distinguish from infallibility. It is certainly a supposable case that the sentiments of the world on moral subjects may undergo a change for the better, bringing them nearer to the proper standard of truth; that a thing may be regarded as innocent in one age which the subsequent age may justly see to be fraught with criminality; that a custom may prevail in one age which a more just application of the principles of the Bible would lead men to abandon; and that an evil may be so intrenched and fortified in one age that it would be hopeless to attempt to remove it then, which, nevertheless, a subsequent age might regard as wholly opposed to the gospel, and wholly at war with the best interests of mankind. It is unnecessary to show that in reference to many wrongs—to duelling, to intemperance, to the slave-trade, to the rights of rulers, to the relation of the church to the state, to lotteries, to civil obligations—the sentiments of the world have so changed as to make it necessary to adjust existing forms and constitutions to those changes; to make such changes as to express the just opinion of a more enlightened age, and not the sentiments of a dark and barbarous generation. A man should not *assume*, therefore, because slave-holding has been at one time tolerated in the church, that *therefore* it is *always* to be tolerated; that because it existed when the Constitution of the church was formed, *therefore* it is to be tolerated always; that because it was once esteemed to be right, it is always so to be esteemed. Nor can it be assumed by any one that because he or his father entered the church with an implied understanding that it was not inconsistent with a good and regular standing in the church, *therefore* it is to be assumed that it is *always* and in all circumstances to be regarded as consistent with a good and regular standing in the church. To deny these principles would obviously be a certain mode of preventing progress, of shutting out the benefit of the light of advancing ages, of petrifying error and sin, and of leaving the church far in the rear, in the questions of morals, of what might be the actual condition of the outside world. What would have been the effect of making such an unchangeable constitution in the time of Abraham, of Jacob, or of David,—in the time of Constantine or Charlemagne,—in the time of Abelard and Duns Scotus? As a matter of fact, however, every *constitution* makes provision for its own modification. The Constitution of the United States may be amended in a specified manner; so may also the Constitution of the Presbyterian church.

It may be asked whether it is desirable or right to be connected with an organization that *seems* to be encumbered in this manner, and which may, by its positive influence, or by declining to act in a right manner, contribute so much to sustain and perpetuate evil in the world.

To this question it is obvious to reply that an organization,—an association under a constitution,—whatever incidental evils may be connected with it, *may be* most powerful for good. It is better for men to act together than to stand alone and to act independently. An organization will bear more efficiently on an evil in removing it than the same number of individuals which compose it would or could if they acted without concerted action; or, in promoting good, will be the more efficient and certain, if it is regulated by constitutional rules or by a constitution, than if it is irregular, fitful, spasmodic. Hence, a church is more efficient in a community than the same number of individuals which compose it would be without an organization; and hence, under the constitutions in the respective States of this Union, and in the United States considered as one, the rights of men are more safe, and the ends of society are better secured, than they could be if there were *no* constitution, or than they could be under an arbitrary rule or in a state of anarchy. In reference to all personal rights of liberty, conscience, property, religion, a *constitution* is invaluable; and the point which men reach in the progress of society is indicated at once by the answer to the question whether the government under which they live is *constitutional* or whether it is despotic. It does not appear that a constitution may not be as valuable in the church as in the state,—in reference to the spiritual as to the temporal interests of men.

It is still a question, however, whether, when a church does not take the stand which it *ought* to do on the subjects of temperance, liberty, humanity, or doctrine, it is better to remain in it, or to leave it,—to attempt to bring it to a right position, or to forsake it and seek another organization,—to endeavour by constitutional changes to induce others to act with us, or to bear an isolated and independent testimony against the evil? Is it (to apply these remarks to the case before us) better to remain in the Presbyterian church, with the views which it has expressed on the subject of slavery, and with the fact before the mind that slavery *does* exist to some extent among its members, and that as yet no efficient discipline has been adopted to detach the church from it, or to withdraw from it on that account, thus, by the act of withdrawing, bearing a decided testimony against the system, and seeking elsewhere the liberty of more decided action in removing the evil? Does not a man, for example, with the views which I have expressed in this paper against slavery, violate his conscience and sin against Christ by lending to the system the *apparent* countenance and support which the fact of his continued connection with the church seems to furnish? Does not such a man, in fact, lend the influence of his name, whatever it may be worth, to the support of the evil, and practically contribute to keep it up in the world?

To these questions I would reply, in general, that there *may* be cases, undoubtedly, where it is a man's duty to separate himself from a corrupt organization, and to bear the testimony against the evil which would result from the fact of leaving such an organization. He is so to act as not to become, by any fair construction, 'a partaker of other men's sins.' If his connection with a church necessarily implies that he approves of the errors which it contains,—if it interferes with freedom of worship, —if the church is wholly heretical or corrupt,—if there is no possibility of reforming it,—if his influence will be wholly lost for good while he remains in it,—if the church is making no progress toward a better state and can not be moved to do it,—then the path of duty might be plain. So Luther and Calvin, acting on such injunctions as those in Rev. xviii. 4, 2 Cor. vi. 16, 17, Isa. xlviii. 20, came out of the Roman communion; and so cases may undoubtedly occur now in which a church is so corrupt as to make a longer continuance in it inconsistent with every sentiment of duty which a man owes to God.

But, in reference to the specific question whether a man holding strong anti-slavery views should, on that account, detach himself from the New-school Presbyterian church, let the following thoughts be suggested:—

(*a*) A man's position as an individual on the subject of slavery, as well as on all other subjects, may be defined and well understood. There is nothing to prevent the full expression of his own sentiments on the subject, either in debate, or in the pulpit, or by the press,—in any way, in fact, that he may choose, public or private. We have seen that in the New-school Presbyterian church, whatever may be true in regard to other churches, the utmost latitude of debate is allowed; the most free expression of opinion on the subject of slavery is consistent with what are understood to be the well-defined views of the church. A man, if wholly detached from this church, could not expect or desire the right of a more full and free expression of opinion; and, in fact, it is presumed that every man's opinions on the subject are well understood. By his connection with the church, moreover, he is not responsible in any way for what another man utters; and so far as the power of bearing testimony is concerned, and so far as a man's influence goes, and so far as he chooses to put forth, alone or in connection with others, any efforts for the removal of the evil, he could not expect or desire greater independence in speaking or acting than he can enjoy in connection with the New-school Presbyterian church. As one illustration of this, I may remark that I pen these sentiments and send them forth with as much conscious freedom, and with as certain a conviction that I shall be free from all molestation in the church on account of them, as I could do if I were wholly unconnected with this church or any other, with as perfect liberty of speech as any professed abolitionist could desire.

(*b*) Again. A man may greatly weaken his influence by detaching himself from a church. There is, indeed, as I have stated before, a point where it becomes a plain matter of duty for a man to withdraw from a corrupt and a degenerate church,—when there is no hope of its reformation, and when his continuing in it must be construed as an approbation of its course; but *up* to that point a man weakens his influence in a good cause by withdrawing from it. He, indeed, bears his testimony against the evil opinions in the church, or its corrupt practices, by separating from it; but he becomes an isolated individual; he loses all the power derived from association; he cuts himself off from what will be regarded, as long as he is connected with the body, as a *right*,—that of endeavouring to exert an influence *on* the body; he deprives himself of all power of effecting a reformation *in* the body itself. Other things being equal, an associated body will listen much more readily to the suggestions of one of its own number than it will to what will be regarded as the intermeddlings of those not connected with it. A man has more influence in his own family than a stranger can have; and he who wishes to reform men should connect himself with them by as many and as tender ties as circumstances, his ability, and his conscience, will allow. Thus, the Redeemer of the world sought to reform men, not by standing at a distance and detaching himself from all connection with the race, but by becoming himself a man and mingling freely with men, even though it subjected him to the charge of receiving sinners and eating with them. It would be easy, were it proper, to refer to *cases* where men have withdrawn from a church because it was worldly-minded, or because it held opinions which they could not sanction, who have lost *all* their influence in that church with reference to its reformation, and whose personal influence in the cause of religion itself has been greatly diminished, if not destroyed, by their assuming an independent position, or by their connecting themselves with another body of Christians.

(*c*) It should be remembered, also, that an *organization* for the promotion of any good object is in itself valuable. A man adds greatly to his own individual strength by associating himself with others. The strand that would be weak in itself becomes strong when twisted with others into a cable; a column that would fall if alone strengthens itself when placed amidst others; a soldier adds greatly to his own strength by being united with others in the discipline of an army; a member of a corporation of any kind greatly adds to his own power by being combined with others. There are numerous things to be done in a community which can be done only by combination and co-operation; and hence men combine in railroad companies, in eleemosynary societies, in missionary associations, in the temperance cause, in insurance companies, in joint-stock operations, and in the anti-slavery cause. The organization which composes the Christian church is one of the best-arranged and the most efficient in the world; and I presume it will be admitted that if that were what it should be, according to its original design, none could be found that would be more serviceable in its power of removing slavery from the world. In itself considered, it is a matter of great importance, if it can be done, to bring *any* church to a just position on this and on all other great moral subjects.

(*d*) Further. The influence of the New-school Presbyterian church is *not* in favour of slavery; and a man does *not* become its advocate and abettor by being connected with that church. If the line of reasoning pursued in this essay is correct, then it is undoubtedly true that, with perhaps the exception of the Quakers, there is no church, in this land or in other lands, whose testimony has been more uniform or more decided against slavery, whose position is better defined, whose aims are more clear, which has pursued the subject so far, or which has gained so advanced a position in regard to the evil. A man, by becoming a member or a minister of that church, practically avows those sentiments as expressing his own views, and places himself in this position before the world. He becomes connected with a body which has never uttered one word, as a body, in extenuation of slavery or in apology for it, and which for more than fifty years, by every form of public testimony, and by a regular train of measures, has declared its purpose to do all that can be done in a Christian manner to 'efface this blot on our holy religion,' and to effect the 'entire abolition of slavery throughout Christendom, and, if possible, throughout the world.' *As a matter of fact*, it is never supposed at the South, nor by any fair construction at the North, that a man is a friend of slavery, or disposed to apologize for it, when he connects himself with that church. He would, at least in many quarters in our country, be much more likely to subject himself, by such an act, to the charge of being an abolitionist; and, if he *wished* to preserve himself from all suspicion of being an abolitionist, he would sooner connect himself with any other of the large denominations in the land than with that.

(*e*) One other remark should be made in reference to the question whether a man holding strong anti-slavery sentiments should remain connected with that body, or should detach himself from it. It is, that he would ultimately gain nothing by connecting himself with any other denomination. There is, indeed, a calm—a most melancholy calm—on this subject *now* in the Episcopal church, in the Old-school Presbyterian church, and in the Baptist denomination. There is a most melancholy zeal for 'conservatism,' and there is much tact evinced in keeping this subject from agitating their churches, and no little self-glorying among themselves that they have been able to exclude the subject from their councils, and, to a great extent, from their pulpits. But this calm will not last always. There is a spirit abroad in this age which demands that this subject shall be discussed, and that the church shall take some definite position in regard to it; and there are men in each of those bodies who will not always be satisfied with 'conservatism' and with a display of worldly wisdom in excluding this great subject from their deliberative assemblies and from their pulpits. There are men who can now with difficulty be restrained by ecclesiastical trammels, and who will not long consent to look with indifference on the fact that three millions of human beings, redeemed by the blood of Christ, are held as property in this Christian land, and denied the rights which God designed should be conferred on all the members of the human family. There are men who will not feel satisfied in their consciences with an effort to deliver the people of India and China and the islands of the sea from idolatry, while their own churches are indifferent to the fact that in their native land there are three millions of human beings deprived of their rights, kept in ignorance, deprived by law of the benefits of public instruction, and subjected to the evils and wrongs which slavery always engenders, and that many even of the members of their own churches sustain a very close and painful relation to the system. Sooner or later—and not very far distant in time—and the sooner the better—the subject WILL be discussed in each of those denominations; and there are reasons, which need not be referred to here, for supposing that it will be done with far more peril than has been experienced in the New-school Presbyterian church. If a man desires *peace*, he had far better remain in the

New-school Presbyterian church, where the subject *has* been discussed and the battle *has* been fought.

But, still, it is a very material question what further *can* be done in that church itself, consistently with the Constitution? Is it *possible* to carry out the principles which have been avowed for fifty years, so as to secure the object contemplated at the outset,—'the entire abolition of slavery,'—the 'effacing of this blot on our holy religion'?

In answer to these inquiries, I observe that the following methods are within the constitutional power of the church; and, IF these were pursued, the entire removal of slavery from the church would be the certain result.

1. The aim or object stated so explicitly in 1818, and repeated and avowed so often since, should be steadily pursued:—'the entire abolition of slavery throughout Christendom, and, if possible, throughout the world.' If *this* avowed aim and object were consistent with the Constitution in 1818, it is consistent now; if it had the sanction of the men who framed the Constitution,—as it did,—then it is consistent that men in the church should lend their sanction to it now. If it was a proper aim in 1818, when slaves in this country were comparatively so few in number, and when the system had extended over so small a part of what now constitutes the United States, it cannot be improper now, when the number has multiplied to three millions,—as large a number as all the freemen of the land when the independence of the country was achieved,—and when tracts of territory have been subjected to the curse larger than any of the kingdoms or empires of the Old

World, with the single exception of Russia. Time, therefore, and the course of events, have done nothing to make this aim *improper*, whatever they may have done to make it more difficult. Yet it is much for a church, as it is for an individual man, to have a definite aim and object, to have its purpose understood, to have a position which is not susceptible of misinterpretation, to have the eye directed to some one great purpose that lies in the path and that is to constitute the goal of its subsequent achievements.

2. The power of *testimony*. No onė can doubt that *this* is constitutional; for the experience of more than fifty years has shown that it accords entirely with the spirit of the Constitution. The only question is whether a sufficient testimony has not been already borne on the subject, and whether it would not now rather hinder than promote the end in view, to reiterate this from year to year.

I have shown what the testimony of the church has been. It has been steady, uniform, consistent. It has been so often repeated, and repeated in language so unambiguous, that the world cannot mistake its import. And yet the power of 'testimony' on the subject may not be exhausted. It is much to keep the facts of the existence of the evil before the public mind; and a 'testimony' borne on any subject by successive bodies of men, though it may not add much to the *argument*, may add much to the moral force of the testimony itself. It is the expression of the deep conviction of a body of men called to look at the subject once more, and once more called to consider the evil and to inquire whether it cannot be removed; it is the voice of living men

added to the admonition of the dead, giving, in addition to their own personal or collected influence, a new utterance to the sentiments of venerated men now in their graves,—men who, if they were to rise again, would utter the admonition in tones still more deep and solemn from the fact that half a century has passed away, and that the evil which pained their hearts while living has been steadily increasing, and that so large a portion of the church still slumbers over it.

At the same time it should be remarked that there is great *power* in bearing testimony against an evil. It is much to call the attention of good men, and bad men also, to their own course of life, or to existing evils with which they may be connected and for the existence of which they may be in any way responsible. It is much to appeal to their consciences, to suggest means for a removal of the evil, to remind them of their own responsibility in the matter, and to urge reasons why the evil should be removed. It was owing in a great measure, if not entirely, to the influence of such testimony, that the society of Friends in this country was enabled to detach itself wholly from slavery and to take that honourable position which they now hold on this subject. Not a blow was struck, not a hard or harsh word was uttered, not a member was excluded on account of his connection with slavery, not an act of discipline was performed. Truth often and long repeated made its way to the hearts of conscientious men, and of their own accord they separated themselves forever from the system, and not a slave is now held by a Quaker in the land.

3. A free *discussion* of the subject is in the power of the church, and is in entire accordance with the spirit of our religion and pre-eminently with the principles of Presbyterianism. It has cost much in the history of religion to establish the position that *every* subject may be *discussed*. It is the result of a long conflict that this point has been reached; but it *has* been reached. It is the result of the greatest struggles in history—it is a consummation sought by ages of conflict—that *all* subjects in morals, in science, in political matters, and in religion, should be open to free inquiry. The point has been gained in this country; it will ultimately be gained throughout the world. This is a settled principle in the New-school Presbyterian church; a principle for which it has strenuously contended; a principle which nothing can compel that church to relinquish. That it is a fixed and settled principle in that church has been manifested in an eminent manner in regard to the very subject now before us; for there is no one subject in relation to which there has been so strong an effort made to secure it from being discussed in our country; there is no one that has been approached with so much difficulty; there is no one in relation to which there would be so many inducements from expediency, conservatism, the desire of peace and union, to pass it by; there is no one of great public interest which other denominations have so studiously avoided; and yet, as I have shown, there is no subject which has been so often, so fully, and so fearlessly discussed in the New-school Presbyterian church as *slavery*.

Now, there is much *power* in removing an evil in mere freedom of discussion. It is much to have it understood that all its bearings may be examined, and much to have it understood that, if it cannot be defended by argument, it is to be abandoned.

More than in any other body in our country, civil or ecclesiastical, is this a power which may be wielded in the New-school Presbyterian church. By the nature of the Constitution of the body, if the system cannot be defended by argument, it is understood that it *must* be abandoned. It is a *possible* and a *supposable* thing that the subject may be so discussed, so clearly shown to be an evil, that those most interested in slavery—those who are now involved in slave-holding—may be induced, of their own accord, to abandon it. Evils have been abandoned by good men, as the result of conviction, even at great pecuniary sacrifices; and it is right and best to assume that this may be done still. Comp. Acts xix. 18–20.

4. In the New-school Presbyterian church it is now a settled principle—so far as the acts of the Assembly go to establish that principle—that 'slaveholding' should be treated as an '*offence*,' in the proper and technical sense of the term,—that is, as a relation subjecting a man to the discipline of the church,—unless he can show that in his case it is rendered necessary by the laws of the state, the obligations of guardianship, and by the demands of humanity. But, by the Constitution, it is supposed that any offence may be reached; that there is a regular process by which a man charged with an 'offence' may have the opportunity to excul-

pate himself, or may be subjected to the discipline of the church.

It is true that there may be 'offences' which, after all, it may not be easy to reach. It may be so difficult to obtain testimony, or there may be so much reluctance to commencing an accusation, or it may be so difficult to reach the 'offence' on the charges of 'common fame,' or the community where the evil exists may be so implicated in the evil, or there may be so much capital invested in it, that it may be difficult to bring it by regular process before the judicatories of the church. It is easy to conceive that this might be the case in regard to the manufacture, the sale, or the use of intoxicating drinks; or the vending of lottery-tickets; or investment of capital in modes of business that involve a violation of the Sabbath; or conformity to the worldly amusements of the theatre, the circus, the opera, or the ball-room. But it is much that in any such case the matter should be clearly defined, and that it should be understood that there *is* a regular way in which the offence might be reached. That there *is* such a way in the New-school Presbyterian church in regard to slave-holding is now a settled principle in that body. It is declared to be an 'offence;' and there is a regular and constitutional method by which *any* 'offence' may be brought before the proper judicatories of the church. Any man may institute a process; and *when* instituted the case would be, or might be, brought in a regular manner before the General Assembly as the highest judicial body in the church. Whoever chooses may as freely institute a process in this case as in any other case; and the Constitution, according to the Report of the Committee of 1856, as adopted by the General Assembly, has *defined* the way by which such a case may be reached and determined.

5. In all communities under a government by a *constitution*, there is an express or implied power to *amend* the constitution if it be necessary. There is no earthly form of government that is to be regarded as necessarily fixed and unchangeable. In all written constitutions there is a power of amendment provided for by the constitution itself; and this is expressly the case in the Presbyterian church. It was apprehended that, in the course of events, there might be found to be defects in the instrument itself; that in the changes of society, in the progress of thought in the world, or in the further investigation of the Bible, it might be found necessary to modify some of the doctrines laid down, or to make new arrangements for the government of the church, or to reach new forms of evil that might spring up in the world. It is, therefore, by no means to be *assumed*, because any practice whatever was regarded as consistent with good standing in the church when the Constitution was formed and adopted, that it is *always* to be so regarded, or that any rights are violated if what was once regarded as consistent with good standing should be afterward, by a regular change in the Constitution, be placed in the list of actions that constitute '*offences*' and subject the offender to the discipline of the church. If, therefore, slave-holding was *ever* regarded as consistent with a fair standing in the

church, or if it has been regarded as an institution to be perpetuated like the relations of husband and wife, guardian and ward, and if any churches were received to the connection of the church under that interpretation, it is perfectly competent for the church so to change the Constitution as to express a doctrine that shall be in accordance with the progressive spirit of the age and with a better interpretation of the word of God; for all churches and church-members have entered the connection under a constitution which provides that such changes may be made. And if, in the changes of opinion in advanced times, it should become the conviction of the church that slave-holding is *not* consistent with the spirit of Christianity and the teachings of the Bible, and if this doctrine had not been expressed with sufficient clearness, the change *ought* to be made. If it were so, it *ought* to be as speedily as possible. On a subject like this there should be no ambiguity or uncertainty in the articles of the church. It should never be susceptible of a plausible suggestion that the constitution of a church *does* sustain slave-holding, or that it regards it as being in any sense whatever on a level with the relation of husband and wife, master and apprentice, guardian and ward. If such is the fair interpretation of the Constitution of the Presbyterian church, or if there is any such ambiguity in it as will give ease and comfort to the conscience of a member of the church who voluntarily and for gain sustains the relation of a slave-holder, the sooner the Constitution is altered or abandoned the better. No constitution ought to exist on the earth which would throw a shield over this gigantic evil, or which would lend the sanction of a Christian organization, or the authority of a Christian rule, or the prestige derived from the Christian name, to the support of an institution under which three millions of human beings are regarded as 'chattels,' and are deprived of the rights of Christian freemen.

For one, however, I do not believe that any change on this subject is necessary in the Constitution of the Presbyterian church. The interpretation of that instrument for a period of not far from fifty years, by which, as we have seen, the system of slave-holding has been condemned, in every variety of language, as utterly 'inconsistent with the spirit of Christianity and with the word of God,' and 'as a blot on our holy religion,' shows that, in the judgment of the great body of the church, there is no need of any change in the Constitution to bring the sin of slave-holding among the acts which subject offenders to the discipline of the church. An undisputed interpretation of an instrument for fifty years ought to be considered as settling its meaning.

6. There remains *one* power still by which the evil may be removed from the church. It is the power by which the Quakers removed it from their body, —the power in the church of voluntarily *detaching itself from the evil*,—such a conviction of the evil as to lead all who are implicated in the system as speedily as possible to *separate* themselves wholly from it.

What I mean by this is, that it is to be held to be *practicable* to induce those who are now implicated in slave-holding, voluntarily and without any coercive measures to separate themselves from the system, so that, under the power of conscience and the influence of a strong public sentiment, the churches may be wholly detached from it.

A few plain considerations may show that this is wholly within the power of the church, and that it is not altogether vain to hope that it *may* occur.

(*a*) One is, that this result has been already brought about, in this way, by one large denomination of Christians,—the Society of Friends. I regard the history of that society, in connection with this subject, as a very valuable and instructive chapter in the records of the church. It illustrates the power of 'testimony,' the power of conscience, and the power of patience and forbearance. It was not by a work of violence that they became free from all connection with slavery; it was a work of peace. It was not by harsh denunciation and unkind words; it was by love. It was not by direct acts of discipline; it was by the power of solemn appeals addressed to the conscience. It was not by coercive measures driven recklessly and rapidly through the body, rending it asunder and producing permanent alienation; it was the slow and patient work of years. Yet it was done. The process was effectual. The last cord that bound the members of that society to the system was severed, and the Society of Friends was the first in modern times which occupied a position which all Christian churches will yet occupy,—the noble and the elevated position of being entirely separate from any connection with slavery. Why should it not be supposed that there is a *conscience* among other Christians as well as among them? Why should it not be supposed that others may hear the voice of entreaty from their brethren as well as they? And why should it not be supposed that patient appeals and remonstrances may be as effectual in other cases as they were in theirs?

(*b*) Sufficient illustrations of this have already occurred in the Presbyterian church itself to lead us to *hope* that it may become more general, and even that it may become universal. It is by no means a very rare thing for ministers and members of the Presbyterian church to emancipate their slaves, even at what seems to be great personal and pecuniary sacrifice. If it were proper, it would be easy for me to mention the names of not a few ministers of the gospel in the New-school Presbyterian church, who, having been born in the slave States, and having inherited slaves, have become impressed with the evil of the system, and have begun early to train their slaves for freedom, and have embraced the earliest opportunity, when it could be done, to emancipate them. Some have done it who are now in the Northern States; some who still minister at the South. In the view of the world, and according to the 'market' estimate of that species of 'property,'—my pen almost refuses to use the word '*property*' in that connection, even for the sake of illustration,—the pecuniary sacrifice has been very great:—in some instances amounting to many thousands of dollars, and in most cases amounting to manifold more than those have been willing to sacrifice for *any* benevolent object who have denounced the system and denounced their brethren. Right as it is that men who hold others in slavery should set them free; proper and Christian as it is that they who have enjoyed the avails of the unrequited labour of others for years should place those whom they have held in bondage in a condition where they may enjoy the avails of their own labour, yet it would be well for us to remember that it may imply some sterner principle to do this than it does merely to denounce the system, and that they who do it may be actually making a sacrifice greater by far than they who denounce them have ever done for any purpose of philanthropy. And yet there have been men—there are men—who are willing to make that sacrifice. What should forbid us to hope that, under the influence of an enlightened sense of duty, the disposition to do this may become more general, and ultimately, and at no distant period, be universal,—so that it may be proclaimed that the Presbyterian denomination, as well as the Friends, are wholly detached from the curse of slavery?—so that there shall be added to the practical testimony against the system that of another entire Christian denomination?

(*c*) It should be added that the number of churches connected with the New-school Presbyterian church in the slave States is comparatively small; and it may be presumed that the number of slave-holders in each of them is small also. There are in the entire New-school Presbyterian church in the United States but three hundred and one churches in the slave States, and but one hundred and ninety-nine ministers, out of one thousand six hundred and seventy-seven churches, and one thousand four hundred and seventy-four ministers, connected with the entire body. There are but seventeen thousand one hundred and forty-six members, out of one hundred and thirty-eight thousand seven hundred and sixty members. The great body of the ministers of the churches, and of the members of the churches, are therefore entirely unconnected with slavery in all its forms and responsibilities. But, further, it may be assumed safely that not one in ten, probably not one in twenty, of the ministers of the Southern churches, are in any form holders of slaves; and, if the latter be assumed as the proportion, then the number of holders of slaves among the ministers would not exceed *ten*, and, for the same proportion, the number of members would not exceed nine hundred. It should be remembered, also, that of the members of the churches a very large proportion is made up of females, of youths of both sexes, and of slaves themselves; and, when these circumstances are taken into the account, it will be seen at once that, while entire accuracy cannot be pretended in the estimate, the actual number of church-members who hold slaves must be an exceedingly small proportion of the whole number. Considering all these facts, probably the whole number of slave-holders in the New-school body is not one thousand out of nearly one hundred fifty thousand members. It would have been very *greatly* to the credit of the Southern churches, and would have placed them in a much more desirable point of view from that which they now occupy, if they had given the information on this subject which the

Assembly which met at Buffalo asked of them, but which they declined to give. It would have appeared, doubtless, and much to their credit, that the number of those who are in any way implicated in slavery at the South is much smaller than is commonly supposed, and that there is among the members of the church in general much more care taken of the slaves, and much more attention to their spiritual good manifested, and much more done among church-members to guard the slaves from the operation of the severe laws in the slave States, than is commonly imagined, and that a large part of the charges alleged against them are calumnies. It would, doubtless, have been found to be true that all that has been said about the kindness of Christian masters is correct, and that the cruelty chargeable on the system in the South is *not* chargeable, to any considerable extent, on the members of the churches. There has never been any measure proposed that gave so favourable an opportunity for removing unjust prejudice, and allaying the bitterness of Northern feeling, and securing the sympathy and confidence of the North, as that measure was. There never has been an instance of a more striking want of wisdom than was manifested in refusing to give that information. Since, however, it was withheld, we can only assume to be true what undoubtedly would have been found to be true on the fullest information:—that the number of slaveholders in the church at the South is VERY SMALL, and that among them there is a good degree of Christian fidelity in bringing them under the instruction of the gospel, and giving them facilities, even in the face of the laws, for reading the Bible and for the free worship of God.

But, *if* thus small, is it a hopeless anticipation that the number may become still smaller? May it not be presumed to be possible that, under the influence of a strong public sentiment, the members of the churches may be induced to detach themselves wholly from the system? Are we not at liberty to presume that there is such a power of conscience, when enlightened by the gospel, that it will lead Christians everywhere ultimately to "do unto others as they would that others should do unto them"? The same difficulty precisely existed in the case of the Quakers; and may it not be presumed that the power of that gospel which among them was made to break the fetters of the slave may do the same thing in other denominations? For one, I do not despair of this. I believe that even *now*, with all that there is in the declared sentiments of many ministers and many editors of papers, and with all the apologies that are made for slavery in the North or in the South, there *is* a silent power at work in the church which *tends* to universal emancipation, and which, under the present operation of things in the Presbyterian church, will sooner or later lead the churches to separate themselves wholly from slavery. It *may be* that, under the pressure of what some regard as severe measures, and of the fact that the subject is constantly agitated in the New-school body, *some* may withdraw from the connection and seek a connection with the Old-school, to renew the strifes which sooner or later MUST come up there; it *may be* that some may become independent, and stand, *as* slave-holding churches, aloof from all others; it *may be* that out of the two Presbyterian bodies at the South there may be formed a Southern organization, with the hope of avoiding the controversy about slavery, and with the hope of enjoying the blessings of the institution unannoyed; but this, I am persuaded, is not the result which is *likely* to occur in the great body of Christian churches in the South. Things *tend* to a better result. There is a spirit abroad in our land and throughout the world which will have its influence there. There is a voice uttered everywhere against slavery so loud and so clear that it will ultimately be regarded. There are evils in the system so inseparable from it that good men will sooner or later detach themselves from it. There is so much in it that is contrary to the Bible, so much that is unlike the spirit of Christ, so much that interferes with the progress of the gospel, so much that tends to debase and degrade, so much in the treatment of others which men would regard as oppressive and wrong if practised toward themselves, their wives, or their children, that the system cannot always be sustained by the conscience of the Christian church. I believe that the New-school Presbyterian church has made a closer approximation to this point than any other organized denomination in the land, that it is a practicable thing for it to become entirely detached from the system, and that that point may be ultimately reached. No good man ought to wish to remain in the church if it could *not* be reached; and, when reached, the New-school Presbyterian church will occupy a position more desirable, in respect to slavery and in respect to its facilities for spreading the gospel, than any other denomination in the land. When that day shall come,—when it shall be announced to the world that every member and minister in the Presbyterian church is himself a freeman, and is *free* from all connection with slavery,—it will be a day of triumph, in respect to the church, equal to that in the fatherland, in respect to liberty, when, in the case of James Somersett, Lord Mansfield pronounced the memorable decision that "*the air of England has long been too pure for a slave*, AND EVERY MAN IS FREE WHO BREATHES IT."* God grant that the time may soon come when that noble principle of law may be proclaimed throughout this whole land! What a triumph for freedom will that be, when that sentiment shall be uttered by a chief-justice of the Supreme Court of the United States!—when the period has arrived in which one occupying that position shall place his name by the side of that of Mansfield!

* Campbell's "Lives of the Chief-Justices of England," ii. 321.

CHAPTER VII.

THE DUTY OF THE CHURCH AT LARGE ON THE SUBJECT OF SLAVERY.

I HAVE thus considered all that I proposed to do in regard to the position of the New-school Presbyterian church on the subject of slavery. I shall finish what I designed, by a few observations on what seems to me to be the duty of the church at large in this land on the subject.

(*a*) My first remark is, that the subject *must* be agitated and discussed in the churches, and it *should* be. It is one in which the interests of religion are so much involved; the church unhappily sustains such a relation to it; it does so much directly and indirectly to sustain the system, and the influence of the church on all moral questions is so great, that it is *right* that the subject should be considered in the churches; *and it cannot be avoided.* What has occurred in the New-school Presbyterian church will and should occur in the Old-school body, in the Episcopal church, in the Baptist churches, and in every large and small denomination in the land. It is not as a *political* subject that it is and should be agitated; but it is because it bears on the cause of religion and is connected with the progress and triumph of Christianity that it is to be and that it ought to be considered. Let politicians, as it may please them, agitate it or not; let political economists, as they may please, discuss it or not; let men consider it or not in regard to the temporal prosperity of our country; yet, in its close and vital connection with religion, the churches have no option in the case, and it will be and should be forced upon them. The question is to be discussed, and should be discussed, whether it accords with the spirit and teaching of the Lord Jesus Christ to uphold a system like American slavery, and whether the churches shall, even by their silence, lend their countenance to a system which now consigns *three millions* of men, women, and children,—a number as great as the Hebrews were in Egypt,—to hopeless bondage.

That the subject will be discussed and agitated in the churches, I think to be clear for these reasons:—

1. The spirit of the age is against slavery; the world is against it. There is a spirit of freedom abroad which there never has been before; and there is a conviction of the essential *wrong* of slavery such as there never has been before. Foreign churches feel more deeply on the subject than they have ever done before; and their appeals and admonitions to their Christian brethren in this country are more earnest and solemn and pathetic than they have ever been; and those appeals are not likely to be fewer in number or feebler in power. In my judgment, they are all proper; and, though they may be sometimes couched in language that seems to be severe, and though they are sometimes met with coldness or thrown back as acts

of intermeddling and impertinence, yet they are the appeals of earnest, sincere, and disinterested Christian men; and they will be repeated, and they will be heard. The apologists for slavery in this land, and the abettors and the sustainers of the system, and all who plead for silence on the subject and for that kind of 'conservatism' which would keep the discussion of the subject out of the churches, set themselves against the firmest convictions of the Christian world, and attempt to occupy a position which cannot long be occupied. It cannot long be a fact that any Christian church will shut its eyes to the abominations of the system, or refuse to consider what can be done to deliver Christianity from any responsibility in upholding so enormous a scheme of oppression and wrong.

2. There are men in all the churches who will not always be silent on the subject. They cannot, by any application of ecclesiastical rules, always be made to suppress the earnest convictions of their souls in regard to the wrongs of the African race; and they will seek utterance for their convictions, and will make their voices heard. It is with great difficulty that such men can now be restrained from giving utterance to their deep convictions of the evil of slavery; with great difficulty that they can be constrained by their silence to seem to lend their countenance to a system which, in their hearts, they deeply abhor. In the Old-school Presbyterian church, and in the Episcopal church, it requires all the power of an efficient and closely-compacted ecclesiastical organization, and all the influence of those who are disposed to hold the power of ruling

in their own hands, to restrain them from giving utterance to their sentiments; and the constraint becomes more galling from year to year. Sooner or later the shackles which fetter such spirits will be broken, and these men will be free. Nothing can be more certain than that the power of public sentiment will be so great as to constrain these bodies to admit this as a proper subject of discussion in their councils; and nothing can be more certain than that the time will come when in the one of these bodies the solemn sentiments of the Assembly of 1818 will be reüttered with a voice that will be heard throughout all the borders of the church, and that in the other such views will become the prevalent views of that body.

That the subject should be thus agitated and discussed, I believe, is in accordance with the spirit of the Bible and the spirit of the age.

(*b*) My next remark is, that the subject of slavery should be everywhere treated as other sins and wrongs are. In the religious literature of the country, in preaching, and in the general public sentiment, this subject should find a place, just as intemperance, Sabbath-breaking, and lotteries, do. It should be introduced into the pulpit, not in its political aspect, but in its bearings on religion, as one of the causes which hinder the progress and triumph of Christianity in the world; and in the same way it should be approached in our religious literature. In any other aspect its discussion has no place in the pulpit, and should have none in the religious literature of our country; but in this respect it *should* have a place, just as any thing else has that hinders the progress of the gospel of Christ. It is undeniable that there must be a great change in our religious literature before this point is reached. No one can fail to perceive that there is now a marked distinction made between this and other evils and wrongs that stand in the way of the gospel. Others are discussed freely. They are approached without the fear of giving offence, and with no desire to palliate the wrong. In the Tract Societies, in the publications of the Sunday-school Union, in the pulpit generally, in a large part of the religious papers of the country, the subjects of intemperance, gambling, lotteries, profaneness, Sabbath-breaking, infidelity, skepticism, are approached without any desire to avoid them, and with no manifested fear of giving offence. They are met as they should be:—not in their political relations and bearings, but in their relation to the salvation of men. But this one great evil,—this system, under which more than three millions of human beings are held in hopeless bondage,—this system, (I speak of the '*system*,' not of the feelings of many who are connected with it,) which treats man not as man, and not as capable of redemption, but as a 'chattel,' as a 'thing,'—this system, which does at least *as much* in this country to hinder the progress of the gospel of Christ, and which involves *as many* violations of the law of God, as either intemperance, gaming, lotteries, Sabbath-breaking, skepticism, infidelity, if not as much as all combined,—is systematically, and on principle, excluded altogether from a large part of the religious literature and a large part of the pulpits of the nation. The slightest allusion to it as an evil is suppressed; books that refer to it as an evil are expurgated, that offence may not be given to the friends and abettors of slavery; and newspapers professing to be religious are projected and issued on the avowed doctrine that the subject is never, in any way, to be alluded to. As a matter of simple fact, also, some of the most powerful of all the organizations in the land for the diffusion of a religious literature exclude this subject entirely; and, though they speak freely of every other sin and wrong, they are wholly silent on this stupendous wrong done to the bodies and souls of men. So far as the influence of those organizations go,—and it is very far,—the practical operation of that influence is to create the impression that this is *not* an evil and a wrong, and that it does *not* so interfere with the salvation of men and the progress of the gospel as to claim the attention of those who are organized into powerful religious associations, and who have vast public funds placed at their disposal for the spread of truth, and for advancing the kingdom of God on the earth.

Now, what the spirit of the age and the spirit of the gospel, as I understand it, demand, is not that the subject of slavery should have any undue prominence in these discussions; not that it should be *forced* into the publications of the Tract Society and the Sunday-school Union; not that it should occupy the sole place in the pulpit; but that *it should be treated just as all other acknowledged evils and wrongs are:*—as contrary to the gospel of Christ, as preventing the salvation of men, as a violation of the spirit of the gospel, and as an evil not to be perpetuated, but to be removed. For one, I am weary —and I am sure that in this I speak the sentiments of many thousands of others—of the perpetual deference shown to the holders of slaves in the pulpit and in the religious literature of the land. I am weary of the care taken, more than in other cases of wrong, to conciliate their favour and to avoid giving them offence. I am weary of the anxiety evinced that every approach to this subject, in so large a part of the literature of the land, should be cut off, and that at so many points we meet this as a matter that is by common consent to be regarded as inapproachable. Why should this be so? How has it happened that in a Christian land mighty organizations have grown up, with vast power and wealth, from which all reference to slavery is excluded on principle, and that it is impossible, through any national organization, though having their seat in the North and sustained chiefly by Northern funds, to utter one word—yes, *one word*—in behalf of the slave?—one word, even to a Christian master, that shall direct his attention to his duty to a fellow-man that he holds in hopeless bondage?—one word to induce him to treat him in all respects as a brother for whom Christ died? It is clear to my mind that a great change should be effected on this subject in the Christian literature of the land, and that in religious newspapers, in the publications of the Tract Society and of the Sunday-school Union, and in all other publications, the subject of slavery should be approached *precisely* as any other admitted evil and wrong is approached.

The same is true in regard to preaching. I would

not have the pulpit depart from its legitimate object. I would not have it placed on the same level with the lyceum. I would not have it a place of vituperative language or of declamation on political subjects. I would not have it a place where party politics should be discussed, or where the opinions of one political party should be defended, or where any political measures should be advocated. I would not have it a place where the interests of one section of the land should be arrayed against another; nor would I have it abused so as to embitter one part of the country against another. I would not have it a place where *disunion* should be advocated; nor would I have it a place where *union* should be advocated at the expense of justice, mercy, humanity, liberty. *The pulpit is a place where every thing should be discussed, in its proper proportions, that bears on the progress of religion and the salvation of men. Every thing* that tends to promote religion should be defended and enforced; *every thing* that hinders it should be rebuked and condemned. There is no subject whatever which bears on the subject of human salvation that can properly escape the notice of the pulpit. There is nothing that can claim to be exempted from that, however shielded and protected by laws and by the established customs of a nation, or however incorporated into civil constitutions, that tends to destroy the soul, or in any way to hinder the progress of the gospel of Christ.

These are plain principles; and they are such as it would seem must meet the approval of all who be'ieve the gospel to be from heaven and to be n essary for the salvation of men, and who believe that the Christian ministry is appointed to defend, illustrate, and enforce all that God has revealed in the gospel. And, if these are true principles, on what pretence can it be maintained that the subject of slavery should never be introduced into the pulpit? Can it be doubted that a system under which three millions of human beings for whom Christ died are held to be 'property' in a Christian land; which deprives them of all civil rights; which appropriates the avails of their labour to the use of others who have no shadow of claim to it; which makes the marriage-tie a nullity; which makes the separation of husband and wife not only a possible but a common thing; which places the time and mode of their worshipping their Maker *entirely* at the control of an irresponsible and perhaps an unprincipled and an infidel master; which regulates every thing, not by the question of the claims of God and the rights of conscience, but by the question how much *labour* can be wrung out of purchased services:—can it be doubted that this system has *something* to do with the progress of the gospel in the world and the salvation of man? Can it be doubted that it will have something to do in affecting the extent to which religion will prevail, and the purity of that religion in the churches? Is it to be held that the manufacture and sale of ardent spirits will have something to do with the progress of the gospel and the salvation of men, and slavery nothing? That the vending of a few lottery-tickets is a matter of sufficient importance to claim the attention of the ministers of religion, and this not? That the amusements of the ball-room, the theatre, and the opera, should engage the earnest prayers and exhortations of the ministers of religion, and that the fact that three millions of human beings are held under such a system can have no claim on the attention of the ministers of Christ? Shall a horse-race, a bull-fight, or even a duel, be deemed of sufficient moment to awaken the indignation and stir the soul of a minister of Christ, and this enormous system of injustice and wrong have nothing to awaken his sympathy and to enkindle his zeal? Is the system of *caste* in India an evil greater than American slavery? Is the voluntary burning of a few widows on the funeral pile, either as an obstruction to the gospel or as actual wrong, to be compared with this system? Is the swinging on hooks or the painful postures of the body in Hindoo devotion an obstruction to the progress of the gospel at all to be compared in extent or in enormity with American slavery? And yet these, all these, are proper subjects, in their places, for the pulpit. These evils may all be described in every pulpit in the land, and for their removal prayers and supplications may be offered everywhere, *because* they hinder the progress of the gospel of Christ The friends of human freedom ask only that the subject of slavery, in its proper proportions, may be treated *precisely* in the same way.

It is true that according to this view, and to every just view of the matter, the subject should occupy a much more prominent place in the pulpit in the region where slavery prevails than where it does not. It is true that God has, in his providence, laid on the ministers of the gospel there a special responsibility, and made it especially their *duty* to endeavour to correct the prevalent public opinion and to bring the gospel to bear on the heart and conscience of the master. It is true that the immediate and direct interest in the matter is with them. And it is true that the ministers of the gospel there have no enviable responsibility, and that they are under temptations which rarely assail good men, even in this world of temptation, *not* to do their duty:—to be silent on the subject, to become the apologists for slavery, or to leave the impression in their preaching that *they* regard the relation as substantially the same as that of husband and wife, and guardian and ward. But what if they do, or do not, their duty in the case? Is the pulpit everywhere else to be silent on the subject? Are we never to consider any evils in the pulpit except such as exist only within the narrow limits of our own parish? Are we never to illustrate the great principles of the gospel of Christ? Are we never to remember that we have a common country, and that slavery affects the North as well as the South? Are we never to remember that slavery is *represented* in the National Legislature? Are we never to remember "those that are in bonds as bound with them"? Are we never to remember that there is on the statute-book of the nation a law most cruel and most iniquitous, and directly contrary to the principles of the word of God, requiring us in the North, in the most harsh and unjust manner, to restore the fugitive slave,—the man who loves liberty as we do,—who seeks it as any one of us would do,—and who has as much *right* to it as any Northern or Southern man has to his own? Are we never to remember that the character of the religion in this land is materially affected by the prevalence of slavery? Are we never to think of the impression which goes forth abroad in regard to our country? And are we never, while we go to convert the nations of Asia and the tribes of the desert, to think of the question which foreign churches and infidels propound to us:—why we, who are so zealous for the deliverance of other people, hold three millions of men and women and children in a condition that cannot be favourably compared with theirs? Why should not I, an American by birth, and having as deep an interest in the honour and welfare of my country as any other man, ever allude to the subject of slavery in the pulpit? Why should not I, in the place where God has ordered my lot, do all that *I* can do to remove every thing that, from this cause and every other cause, hinders the progress of the gospel of Christ? I would not, indeed, have this or any other subject made a *hobby* in the pulpit. I would not have ministers of the gospel go out of their way to discuss it. I would not have it discussed in its political or sectional bearings. But I would have it discussed *precisely* as any other subject is discussed in the pulpit:—never drawn in needlessly; never avoided when it comes fairly in the way in illustrating the teachings of the word of God.

(*c*) One other thing should be done. The churches should *detach* themselves from all connection with slavery. They should be wholly separated from it. They should stand apart from it. If it is to be maintained in our country, it should not be by the churches of Christ; if it is to find advocates and defenders, it should not be there. The church, in relation to this, should occupy the same position which it does in relation to duelling or to gambling; the same which it seeks to occupy in regard to intemperance and worldly amusements,—to the theatre and the ball-room. If the practices connected with those things are to be continued in the world, it is not to be by the aid of the Christian church; if they are to find abettors, it is not to be in the pulpit. Whether they can live or not without the aid of the Christian church may be a question for those interested in them to determine; but, if they *do* live, it is to be without its countenance and support. They must look for their patrons elsewhere; and, whether they live or not, the friends of those things should not be able to rely on the support of the church. If they cannot live, it is to be because they have not vitality enough to sustain them when detached from the church of Christ.

So it is to be in regard to slavery. The church is to *detach* itself from it wholly and forever. It is to withdraw from the system, and, so far as the support of the system is concerned, it is to be left to itself. If it has vital power of its own,—if it meets the wants of a worldly society,—if it so promotes human happiness, so contributes to industry, good morals, and the happiness of social life, as to be needful to the world,—it is to live by its own vital power, and not by life infused into it by the church of Christ. If it would die should it be separated from the church, it is to be suffered to expire. But whether, outside of the church, it *is* to live or to die, it is to be suffered to show what it *is*, and what it *would be*, if it derived no countenance from the church of God. Like every thing else which has no proper connection with Christianity, it is to be suffered to stand by itself, looking for no countenance whatever from the organization which Christ has set up with reference to his kingdom on earth. If it can stand by itself, let it stand; if it cannot stand, let it fall, not leaning for its support on the redeemed church of God.

Assuredly the church might thus be detached from slavery; and in doing it, it would interfere with no man's rights, it would abridge none of the liberties which men may claim. If they choose to keep up the institution of slavery, it is a question for *them* to settle; but, in doing it, in the name of all that is sacred and pure and holy and free, let them not be able to plead the authority or to rely on the aid of the church of Christ.

How the church *can* detach itself from all connection with slavery is indeed a question for each one of the denominations of Christians to determine for itself: but it can be done; it must be done; it will be done. The example of the Quakers shows that it can be done; every thing in the onward progress of events shows that it will be done. It *may* be done by each denomination peacefully. By prayer, by patience, by exhortation, by testimony, by the exercise of charity and forbearance mingled with Christian fidelity, by a growing conviction of the evil, by free discussion, by a deeper spirit of piety, the work may be done,—done by each denomination for itself; done by each family for itself; done by each individual for himself. In accordance with existing laws in the churches, or by such modifications of those laws as the age requires, it may be done in each denomination in such a way that there shall be no violence, and that no man's rights shall be invaded. Is there any *necessity* that slavery should exist in the church? Is there any such affinity in the church for the system that it cannot move through the world without invoking the aid of slavery? Is it a matter of fact that the church in its past history has attached to itself the institution of slavery, and that it has lent its aid to sustain it from age to age? Is it a matter of fact that the church at large is now encumbered with this system, and that it contributes its support and lends the *prestige* of its name to keep it up in the world? Far from it. The church at large, as has been shown, has not been the sustainer and abettor of slavery; the church at large is not now. This is true of the Established church and the Dissenting churches of England; of the Presbyterian churches of Scotland; of the Reformed church in France and Switzerland and Holland; of the Lutheran churches on the continent of Europe; of the Greek church, the Nestorian church, and the Roman Catholic communion; and, it is believed, of *all* the missionary churches throughout the world. The practical supporters of slavery in the Christian church are found only in the churches in the Southern States of this Union; and can it be believed that it is *impossible* for those churches to detach themselves from the system, and to stand before the world on a level with the other churches of the Redeemer? Are they doomed to a hopeless condition on this subject? Are they forever to feel the withering, blighting, paralyzing, miserable effects of slavery?

The church will be free. The time will come when in all this land every church shall be wholly and forever *detached* from all connection with slavery. Nothing can be more certain than this. The spirit of the age demands it; the religion which is professed in this land will ultimately secure it; the spirit of our civil institutions will make this certain in the church; the onward progress of liberty among the nations will compel the churches, if they will save the world from infidelity, to detach themselves altogether from slavery. Nothing can be more certain than that the period *will* arrive when in all this land there shall not be one church which will retain any connection with slavery; when there will not be found one minister of the gospel to defend the system, to apologize for it, or to maintain that it is on the same level as the relation of parent and child, husband and wife, guardian and ward. No man can believe that the fair application of the principles of the gospel of Christ would perpetuate the system. In fact, even those who now apologize for it, and who maintain that the system is not inconsistent with the Bible, in general admit most freely that the full influence of Christianity would remove it; and they only ask us to allow them to *make* such an application in their own way, and not to precipitate by hasty action what would most certainly be effected by time and by the slow but certain influence of the religion of Christ.

CHAPTER VIII.

THE CONSEQUENCES OF A PROPER POSITION BY THE CHURCH AT LARGE ON THE SUBJECT OF SLAVERY.

SUPPOSING, then, that all the churches in this nation were wholly detached from slavery, the following consequences would follow:—

1. The system itself could not long be sustained. There is not vital energy enough in the system to maintain itself in this age of the world if it received no countenance from the Christian church, and if that church were arrayed against it. There is no organized system of evil which could maintain a permanent position in this land if the whole church were arrayed against it, and if all the moral power of the church were employed to discountenance and remove it. If each of the great denominations of Christians in the land should first detach itself wholly from the system, and should thus bring the power of its own example to bear upon it, and if, in a proper way, the power of the church, through the pulpit, the press, and the private sentiments and lives of its members, were brought to bear upon it, no one can believe that the system would long exist. It is thus in the power of the church, if it would, to secure, at no distant period, the entire abolition of slavery in this land; and, having this power, it must be held responsible for its exercise. And if it

be a fact that the church *has* the power, it is a most humiliating and painful reflection that that power is *not* exercised, and that this monstrous system *can* look for its support in any way to the church of God.

2. If the church were detached wholly from slavery, it could engage *consistently* in the work of spreading the gospel around the globe. It is difficult now to make it *appear* consistent for a church that aids and abets slavery to engage seriously in the work of missions. It is not easy to make it appear why the church should make war on *caste* in India, or why it should show peculiar zeal to carry the gospel to China, or why it should seek to convert the South Sea Islanders, when it sustains an institution itself not *less* baneful in its influence than any which exists in heathen lands. And it is difficult to make it appear how this same gospel shall commend itself to the heathen abroad, when it shall come to be fully understood by them that the churches which show such zeal for their conversion lend their influence to sustain a system by which three millions of human beings are held to be '*property;*' are subject to all the conditions of property, and are deprived of all the rights and privileges which Christians in their efforts to spread the gospel seek to impart to the people of other lands. It would be easy for the people of other Christian lands to reproach us for inconsistency in our zeal to spread the gospel among the heathen; and it would *not* be easy to reply to the reproach. With what consistency, it might be asked, *can* a nation engage in the work of missions to the heathen which systematically and on principle holds three

millions of human beings in slavery? What is the *kind* of religion which such a people would seek to introduce among the heathen and to substitute for the forms of superstition and idolatry which prevail there? Would they seek to propagate a system of religion which maintains that it is right for the powerful to subjugate the weak?—which teaches that those for whom Christ died may be bought, and sold, and tasked, as beasts?—which deprives a large portion of the population of the country where it prevails of all right to the avails of their own labour, and consigns them to hopeless bondage? And what would be the *advantage* of substituting a religion where such views and purposes are avowed, for those systems which now actually prevail in heathen lands? How much *better* is the condition of the African slave in the United States than the condition of the inhabitants of China, or India, or Arabia, or Armenia, or Turkey? What advantage would there be in introducing into those lands a system of religion which would make it certain that a large part of those who should dwell there would be consigned to hopeless bondage?—where, to keep down the innate love of freedom and the aspirations for liberty, all the sanctions of the new religion would be required, and where it would be held and taught that one portion of mankind is to be regarded as 'chattels' and as 'property,' and to be degraded and debased by slavery *forever?* Even the heathen could see that it violates the fundamental principles of their own nature to attempt to spread a religion which proclaims such a doctrine. There is a teaching of their own nature,—of the Author of their being,—degraded as they are, which will proclaim *to them* that such a religion cannot be from heaven; and, could the matter be fairly proposed to them, they would not hesitate long between retaining their present systems, debasing as they are, and receiving one which would make debasement, ignorance, and degradation perpetual.

And who of those who have gone from this country as missionaries to the heathen would *dare* on heathen soil to advocate the views of the friends of slavery, or to maintain that the system of oppression and wrong which exists here would be made perpetual by religion, and that the religion which they have come to propagate would doom one portion of the population of every land to hopeless bondage? Not thus inconsistent are men when they go to preach the gospel among the heathen; and among all the missionaries of the gospel in pagan lands there are probably none who are not enemies of slavery; none who would *dare* to inculcate there the doctrines so often avowed in our own land,—that slavery is a 'patriarchal' institution, that the New Testament is not unfavourable to it, that it is not inconsistent with the spirit of the gospel of Christ, and that it is to be diffused and perpetuated as a relation of substantially the same kind as that of husband and wife, parent and child, guardian and ward. Soon, very soon, and justly too, would such apostles be given to understand, in every heathen land to which they might choose to go, that their services would not be needed there, and that their teachings would not be appreciated there. Whatever might be the evils of their own systems, they would say that a religion like this could not be from God.

3. The detaching of the church from slavery would remove one of the chief hinderances which now prevent the spread of the gospel in the world. I suppose that no one can be so blinded as not to perceive—and I would hope that there are few so uncandid as not to admit—that slavery in our country presents many very serious obstacles to the propagation of the gospel; in other words, that it is much more easy to propagate the gospel amid free institutions than it is where a large portion of the population is held in helpless bondage,—their time, their skill, the avails of their labour, and even their persons, being wholly the '*property*' of others,—and where the other portion sustains the relation of masters or owners, with all the acknowledged bad influence on industry, economy, and general manner of living, resulting from that relation. No one could maintain that, under any circumstances, the institution of slavery was a *desirable* one to aid in the propagation of the gospel, or that it furnished any facilities for the reception of the gospel by a slave himself; and as little could it be maintained that the natural effect of the system on the master would be favourable on his part to the reception of the gospel of Christ. No one could be so mad as to suppose that the laws in respect to slavery in this country furnish any special facilities for the propagation of the gospel among slaves, unless he were prepared to maintain that the laws of the Roman empire were specially favourable to the spread of Christianity; and no one can suppose that the effect of that system of laws, and of the institutions existing under

them, is favourable to the reception of the gospel by the masters or owners of slaves, unless he is prepared to maintain that the worst edicts of despotism in the Roman empire had some magic power in disposing the hearts of those who enacted them to embrace a religion of purity, justice, and peace. No one could maintain that, in order to the rapid and certain spread of the gospel in the world, it would be *desirable* to anticipate its march among the nations by the establishment of just such a system of slavery as exists in the slave States of the Union, and to put the minds of men in heathen lands in the same position absolutely and relatively which exists in the case of American masters and African slaves. If any one were to maintain this, it would be difficult to see on what basis an argument could be conducted on the subject, or how there could be any admitted principles in common which would lead to a certain conclusion.

As little would it be maintained, I apprehend, that the religion which actually exists in the mind either of the master or the slave, so far as it can in any way be traced to slavery, or so far as it is modified by slavery, is the most desirable kind of religion, or is the best type of Christianity in the world. There *are* owners of slaves who are Christians. No one can reasonably doubt this; no one need be tempted by any rational views of the influence of slavery to deny it. But it would be weakness and folly to maintain that their piety is in any sense the effect of slave-holding, or that the relation is not an unfavourable one to the propagation of the gospel, or that the feelings naturally produced by slavery on the master himself and on his family are unpropitious to the spread of Christianity. The master is pious not as the result of the system, but in spite of it; and he maintains the ascendency of piety in his own bosom not by any natural influence of slavery in engendering and cultivating religious principles, but amid many difficulties which spring out of the system, and which tend to mar his religion. It is not desirable for a Christian, any more than it is for any other man, to be intrusted with the irresponsible power of a slave-holder; for his family, it is not desirable that they should be trained up under the influence of the passions and habits which the system of slavery engenders. Multitudes of pious parents feel that, in respect to the influences of religion, it is *not* desirable to train up their children amidst the institutions of slavery; and not a few, on this account, seek a home where slavery is unknown,—at the North. Multitudes of Christians feel that they *as* Christians would breathe more freely, and could more easily maintain the life of religion in the soul, if it were not for the constant bad influence on their own hearts resulting from the system of slavery.

4. The advantage which would result in spreading the gospel through the world if the church were wholly detached from slavery may be seen from another point of view. One of its regular and unavoidable effects, wherever it exists, is to prevent any great efforts for diffusing the gospel either there or elsewhere. The labouring part of the population, which is made up of slaves, can contribute nothing to the cause of benevolence; for they

own nothing,—not even themselves or their children; and little or nothing of the avails of their labour can be contributed to the cause by their masters; for it is all needed to support their owners, and the families of their owners, who do *not* labour. What is the amount of money which is annually raised in the churches of this land where slavery exists for the purposes of Christian benevolence? What proportion of the funds for the spread of the gospel in pagan lands, —for the preaching of the gospel in the destitute parts of our own country,—for the circulation of the Bible,—for a religious literature,—comes from the slave-holding States of this nation? What proportion of the missionaries now in heathen lands have gone from the slave States? As compared, for instance, with Christians in the free States, what are Christians in the slave States doing for the spread of the gospel in their land or in other lands? What does South Carolina do as compared with Massachusetts? What does Virginia do as compared with New York? And yet, so far as can be seen, the sole reason why they are not doing as much in this great cause is to be traced to slavery. Have they not a climate as genial, and a soil as fertile, as the dwellers in the North? Have they not natural advantages for commerce and manufactures equal to the North? Is the climate of South Carolina more severe and stern than that of Massachusetts, or is the soil naturally more forbidding and repellant? Is Virginia sterile and barren by nature, or has it been made so by slavery? Are Pennsylvania and New York more fertile by nature, or have they been made more productive by the labours of freemen?

Is the fact that constant streams of beneficence flow out to bless the world from the New England States, and from New York, owing to the Northern soil? And is the fact to be traced to difference of climate or soil that, as our population rolls on toward the Western ocean, these streams of benevolence break out in the wilderness as a Northern population spreads over them, in Ohio, Indiana, Illinois, Iowa, and that all is still comparatively a desert and a waste where a Southern population diffuses itself over Alabama, and Arkansas, and Texas? It is owing to other causes. And the sole and sufficient reason of all this difference is, that the one portion is blessed with a freedom which accords with the gospel and which tends to develop the gospel in the soul of man, and that the other is cursed with a system of slavery which is a violation of every principle of the gospel and which tends to dry up every fountain of benevolence in the human soul. The one makes a country rich, and prompts to the right use of riches; the other makes a country poor, and at the same time puts it out of its power to do what a free population may do, and adds this further curse that it makes the population indifferent to it.

5. The effect of detaching the churches from all connection with slavery would be further seen in respect to the religion of the slaves themselves.

No one need deny that there are slaves, perhaps in large numbers, who are Christians. No one need deny that there are many who are now Christians who would not have been if it had been their lot to remain in Africa, or if their ancestors had not been removed, even amid so much that was cruel and wrong, from their native land, and doomed to servitude. No one need deny that there are slaves who are, in all respects, eminent examples of the power of true religion in transforming the heart, enlightening the mind, enabling its possessor to bear trials with patience and resignation; and of its power in making them faithful in the relation which they actually sustain in life. But, while this is admitted, still, such questions as these are to be asked:—Is such religion to be regarded as in any manner the consequence or the legitimate fruit of slavery? Is this the general type of the religion of slaves? Is the system such as is adapted to produce and foster this kind of religion? If it is, then should not we all regret that *our* lot is not that of slavery, and that *our* children are not nurtured under its benevolent arrangements?

Conceding, however, all that I have now conceded in regard to the fact that there *are* slaves who are truly and eminently pious, and who in their very humble condition furnish an example which ought not to be lost on their masters, yet the following things will be admitted to be true by all who know any thing of the religion of slaves.

(*a*) The system is *unfavourable* to religion. It has no provisions that are adapted to promote religion; it has none of which Christianity can avail itself in propagating itself in the world. The whole system is an obstruction—a hinderance—to the progress of the gospel. Slaves, according to the system, are not their own; their time is not their own; the avails of their labour are not their own; their wives and children are not their own; their Sabbaths are not their own;

their bodies are not their own; their souls, so far as they can be made to subserve the interests of their masters, are not their own. They are dependent on others for leave to assemble together for the worship of God; for time to worship God in their own 'cabins;' for the kind of religious teachers, if any, which they may have; for even the use of the Sabbath as a day of rest and devotion. The system in this land contemplates, by a provision which all must admit to be necessary if slavery is to be perpetuated, that slaves shall *not* be taught to read, and that it shall be regarded in law and in fact as an act of felony for any one, unless it be their masters, to teach them to read the word of God. Their religion, therefore, is to be a religion of restraint and dictation,—a religion without the Bible,—a religion in fetters and chains. How *can* the free and true spirit of Christianity be developed in such circumstances?

(*b*) Though there may be true religion among slaves, yet, from the nature of the case and as a matter of fact, it must be a very imperfect development of the nature and power of true religion. It cannot be based on intelligence, when the reading of the Bible is prohibited; and it must be, to a great extent, a religion not of principle, but of feeling. There may be fervour, warmth, ardour; there may be excitement and noise; but all the accounts of the actual religion of slaves agree with what from theory we should infer must be the case:—that their religion, though it may be sincere and simple, is of the humblest order. The general impression of those best acquainted with it, as well as the testimony of travellers, goes to establish the fact which must be inferred from the nature of the case, that, while there are many professors of religion among slaves, there is very little true piety; that many of them are strangers to it altogether; and that in the cases where it does exist it is of the very humblest order. How can it be otherwise?

(c) In the nature of the case, also, their religion will be connected with a very low sense of the obligations of morality. As a general thing, can *any* reliance be placed on the virtue, the truth, the honesty, the fidelity, even of professedly Christian slaves? *Is* there, in fact, any such reliance reposed in them? There may be honourable exceptions; but they *are* exceptions. The whole arrangements in slave-holding communities proceed on the supposition that *no* reliance can be placed on the honesty, the faithfulness, the truth, even of the members of the churches who are slaves. Their testimony is not admitted in courts of justice; no confidence is placed in them that they will be faithful to their daily task without the presence of a master or an overseer; every thing in a house and around a house is placed under lock and key; every precaution is taken to guard them from escaping; and there is a constant fear *expressed* that even the best of their slaves may be excited to murder their masters. They are systematically, and on principle, prohibited from learning to read,* and, even when

* "All meetings or assemblages of slaves, or free negroes or mulattoes mixing or associating with such slaves at any such meeting-house, or any other place, in the night, or *at any school or schools for teaching them reading or writing either in the day or night*, under what-

this provision is disregarded and they are taught to read, the most vigilant care is supposed to be necessary to prevent their becoming acquainted with those writings which acquaint men with their rights, and which tend to elevate them in the scale of moral being. Even among Christian slaves, the masters would not *dare* to allow the ordinary books on Christian morals to be circulated among them. Further: in the very condition of the slave, even under any influence of religion that can be brought to bear upon him, there is every possible *inducement* to dishonesty, falsehood, deception, and degradation in every form in morals. The slave, in spite of any views of religion which he has, *steals*:—that is, *steals* in the sense which the master puts on his act, but not in his own view of the matter; for his master has defrauded him of his personal liberty and of the avails of his own labour, and why should he *not* take back for his own comfort a part at least of that which has by force and violence been taken from him? But what is such a religion worth? How little does it approach the view which we ought to take of the fair influence of Christianity! How little is there in the religion of slaves to commend Christianity as a religion of purity, truth, and virtue! What idea would men obtain of Christianity if they were to learn it from the moral conduct of slaves? How *can* Christianity ever be so developed to show what it is, and what it is designed to be, under such a system as that of American slavery?

---

ever pretext, shall be deemed and considered an unlawful assembly."—1 *Rev. Code of Virginia*, 434, 435.

(*d*) There is nothing that can be introduced *into* the system that will serve to correct and remove these evils, and elevate the Christian slave to what a Christian should be. To him is assigned a very humble place in the house of God, even under the best circumstances; he has no control over his own time; he is not a master in his own family; he is held as the absolute property of another; and he can devote neither his skill, nor his influence, nor his time, nor the avails of his labour, in any proper sense, to the promotion of the cause of religion; for all of these are the property of his master.

(*e*) As a matter of fact, these three millions of slaves, even if they were all Christians, could do nothing for the diffusion of Christianity in the world. They are *the* labourers of the South,—those on whom the South depends for its wealth. They constitute one-third of the whole population, and, in the theory of slavery, they labour to support the other portion of the population. Yet what do they do, what can they do,—what could they do if they were all Christians,—in spreading the gospel of Christ? Not one of them could go to heathen lands to preach the gospel; not one of them, on principle, has one cent that he can call his own, to give in order to send a tract, a missionary, or a Bible, to heathen lands. Now, take the same number of *labourers* at the North, and compare the influence which they may have, and do have, in spreading the gospel. As a matter of fact, no small part of the preachers of the gospel come from that portion of the population; no small part of all the missionaries of the world are raised up from among that class;

no small part of all the contributions to the Tract Society, the Bible Society, the Sunday-school cause, and the missionary cause, come from that class of men at the North. The portion of the community which in the aggregate does most for the support of those institutions are the *labourers* of the North,—the men who are doing substantially the work of the slaves of the South in respect to productive industry; while not one farthing, so far as is known, ever came into the treasury of a tract society, a Bible society, a Sunday-school society, or a missionary society, *from all the three millions of slaves at the South,*—AND NEVER WILL. Is there nothing in this to hinder the progress of the gospel? What *ought* not the labouring population of the whole Southern portion of this Christian land to contribute for the spread of religion in the world?

From such considerations as these, I infer that the existence of slavery presents one of the most formidable obstacles to the extension of pure Christianity in our land; I infer that its removal would at once facilitate, to an extent which no man can estimate, the conversion of the world to the Saviour.

6. If slavery were removed from the church, one of the most plausible arguments in favour of infidelity would be taken away. I have already referred to the fact that slavery exists in the church, and that it is defended by the ministers of the gospel as a 'patriarchal' institution, and as not contrary to the spirit of the New Testament. These facts constitute *one* of the arguments against Christianity on which the rejecters of the Bible rely. I have already endeavoured to show that if a professed

revelation *did* countenance slavery as a desirable institution, and place it on the same level with the relation of husband and wife, parent and child, guardian and ward, it would be impossible to show that it *could* be a revelation from heaven. It would so impinge on great principles of our nature; so contradict the essential laws of our being, and be so at war with all our notions of the rights and the dignity of man and the suggestions of humanity, that it would be impossible to commend it to the mass of men as a communication from God. This would be rendered more and more certain as the world makes progress in civilization and freedom, and as the institutions of philanthropy become more and more established. No pretended revelation could secure a permanent hold on the faith of mankind which should declare polygamy lawful and proper; none that would encourage war; none that would defend the doctrine that there are different original races of men; none that could be fairly employed in defence of duelling, piracy, or freebooting. A revelation, to secure the faith of mankind, must be in all respects *abreast* of what the race will ever come up to in science, in liberal arts, in the arrangements that tend to promote the welfare of mankind, and in just notions of liberty and of the rights of man. It must do more than this. It must be *in advance* of the ordinary progress of society in these things; and the moment it could be proved that society, in any of these respects, is in advance of the pretended revelation, or that it would check and restrain the race in its onward progress, that moment the faith of men would begin to falter in regard to the pretended revelation; that moment it would lose its hold never to be regained.

Such I believe to be the case in regard to slavery. The world is taking its position in respect to the rights of man. There is no principle that is better established in English law than that pronounced by Lord Mansfield,—that the air of England 'is too pure for a slave, and every man is free who breathes it.' There is no one principle that is becoming more firmly rooted in the conviction of mankind than that slavery is contrary to the law of nature; that it is a violation of the inalienable rights of a human being; that there cannot be property in man in the sense in which there is in a horse or an acre of ground; that man cannot be deprived of liberty except for crime, and then only in due course of law; that a human being cannot be bought and sold as an article of merchandise may be; that every one has a right to the avails of his own labour; and that the relations of husband and wife, and parent and child, are too important and too holy to make them liable ever to be severed to promote the pecuniary advantage or to minister to the indolence of others. Among Christians the conviction is becoming more and more rooted in the understanding and the heart that no institution or arrangement in society *can* be right which refuses instruction to any human being, and that any system is and must be wrong which makes it necessary for the support of the system to withhold the Bible from *any* one for whom the Redeemer died.

From these positions the world is never to go

back. Whatever changes in society may occur, these points are fixed. No changes in human belief are in the direction of a retrograde course on these points; all future changes will tend more and more to rivet these convictions on the hearts of men. Advocates for slavery, and apologists for slavery, in the church and out of it, may assume it as certain that these are to be regarded as permanent doctrines in the faith of mankind, and that these doctrines will ultimately pervade the globe. England will never go back from the opinion expressed by Lord Mansfield; and the 'common law' of the world will not be so changed as to declare that slavery *is* consistent with the laws of nature and the fundamental doctrines of the rights of man. "It is repugnant to reason and the principles of natural law that such a state should subsist *anywhere*."*

With equal certainty, the advocates of slavery, and the apologists for slavery, may lay it down as a fixed principle that no book pretending to be a revelation from God can maintain its hold on the faith of men which is not, by fair interpretation, understood to maintain these doctrines, or which can be shown to advocate slavery. It is an objection strongly urged by Mr. Newman (Phases of Faith) against the Bible that it *does* defend slavery: perhaps the only instance in which this has been alleged by any objector against the truth of Revelation from Celsus to the present time. The fact that *he* has urged it shows that infidels would be glad to avail themselves of this as a weapon against revealed

* 1 Blackstone, 423.

religion if they could; the manner in which he has done it is such that it would be impossible to remove the objection if the Bible in fact sustained slavery; while, at the same time, the fact that the objection has not been insisted on before by infidels may be referred to as an incidental proof that the Bible is *not* in favour of slavery. It is obvious, however, that all those ministers of religion who maintain that slavery is an institution sanctioned by the Bible become, in this respect, helpers and allies of such men as Mr. Newman, and put an argument into the hands of infidels which it would not be possible to refute, and no stronger argument against the divine origin of the Bible could be urged. The world, in its advanced periods,—in the position to which it is tending,—would not receive any book as a revelation from God which could be fairly appealed to sustain American slavery. That fact, if it were a fact, would neutralize every argument in favour of the book; for it would be alleged, and in a manner to which no reply could be made, that men may be mistaken in regard to the external evidences of a professed revelation from God, but that they cannot be mistaken ultimately in regard to the deep-seated principles of justice, equity, and humanity, which the Author of our being has implanted in the human soul. Of one thing, therefore, the Christian church may be assured:—that mankind will not ultimately receive, as a revelation from God, *any* book which, by a fair interpretation, sustains the institution of slavery. Every man who asserts that that *is* a fair interpretation of the Bible does just so much to make infidels; every one who maintains that position puts a weapon into the hand of infidelity which can never be wrested from it. We *cannot* answer the argument for infidelity drawn from this source, if we admit that slavery is authorized by the Bible, any more than we could answer the argument if the Bible, by a fair interpretation, justified polygamy, theft, highway robbery, or piracy.

But let slavery be removed from the church, and let the voice of the church with one accord be lifted up in favour of freedom; let the church be wholly detached from the institution, and let there be adopted by all its ministers and members an interpretation of the Bible—as I believe there may be and ought to be—that shall be in accordance with the deep-seated principles of our nature in favour of freedom, and with our own aspirations for liberty, and with the sentiments of the world in its onward progress in regard to human rights, and not only would a very material objection against the Bible be taken away,—and one which would be fatal if it were well founded,—but the establishment of a very strong argument *in favour* of the Bible as a revelation from God would be the direct result of such a position. For then it might be urged that the Bible not only appeals to great principles of our nature as God has made us, but it might be asked, in a manner to which no infidel could reply, how it happened that the Bible, in this respect, was so far in advance of the age in which it was written. How came sentiments to be incorporated in a book penned in Judea, so entirely in accordance with what would ultimately be the views of the most enlightened and civilized portions of the world, and so far in advance of the prevailing sentiments of the age in which it was written? How came it to utter such sentiments in favour of human freedom and the rights of all men at a time when the universal voice of the world was in favour of slavery? How can this fact be *better* accounted for—how can it be accounted for at all—except on the supposition that the writers of the New Testament were taught from on high, and were led by a Spirit superior to their own, to utter sentiments directly the reverse of the prevailing opinions of their own age, but in entire accordance with what would *become* ultimately the sentiments of the world and enter at last into the laws of all civilized nations? "I defy any man," says the author of the 'Eclipse of Faith,'* "to discover, in any age, or in any nation, any considerable body of men who breathed a word of disapprobation of slavery *as such* till Christianity came into the world; nor then, except among those nations that have been brought into contact with it. The apathy of all the nations of antiquity, and all nations not Christian at the present day,—the utter unconsciousness of the best moralists of antiquity of there being any harm in slavery,—confirms the conclusion that the origination of right sentiment on this subject has been the work of Christianity. Nothing really avails against this gigantic evil except the influences that have abolished both the slave-trade and slavery among ourselves; that is, a deep impression that slavery is utterly opposed, if not to the letter, yet

* Defence of the "Eclipse of Faith," p. 168.

to the entire spirit, of Christianity, and that it and the gospel cannot coexist in perpetuity. It may last long, for human cupidity is not more easily subdued than slavery; but where Christianity enters the fray is sure to begin, and will never terminate but with the extinction of slavery itself." At the very time when the noble sentiments which occur in the New Testament in favour of the equality of man and the claims of humanity and human rights were uttered by the apostles and disciples of the Saviour,—sentiments universally admitted to be opposed to slavery and to be such as would, if fairly applied, bring slavery everywhere to an end, except by the *few* Christian ministers and members of the churches who endeavour to defend the institution from the Bible, and who aim to place the relation on the same basis as that of husband and wife and guardian and ward, and by a *few* infidels (if there should be found enough in addition to Mr. Newman to justify the use of the word '*few*,' as applied to them) who have urged it as an objection to the Bible that it sanctions slavery,—the following facts show what was then the current opinion on the subject in the most enlightened nations of the world:—"The custom of exposing old, useless, or sick slaves in an island of the Tiber, there to starve, seems to have been pretty common at Rome; and whoever recovered, after having been so exposed, had his liberty given him by an edict of the Emperor Claudius, in which it was likewise forbidden to kill any slave merely for old age or sickness. It was the professed maxim of the elder Cato to sell his superannuated slaves at any price rather than maintain what he esteemed a useless burden.

"The *ergastula*, or dungeons, where slaves in chains were forced to work, were very common all over Italy. Columella advises that they be always built under ground, and recommends it as the duty of a careful overseer to call over every day the names of these slaves, like the mustering of a regiment or ship's company, in order to know presently when any of them had deserted.

"Nothing [was] so common in all trials, even of civil cases, as to call for the evidence of slaves, which was always extorted by the most exquisite torments. Demosthenes says that, when it was possible to produce for the same fact either freemen or slaves as witnesses, the judge always preferred the torturing of slaves as a more certain evidence."*

"The master had the entire right of property in the slave, and could do just as he pleased with his person and life, his person and his earnings. In regard to the power of life and death, it was contended, the master could use the slave for any purpose that suited his own pleasure. He could punish him, put him to pain and torture, and—free from all obligation to give account of his own actions—could put him to death in any way that pleased him."†

Slaves were liable to every kind of torture; and cruel masters sometimes kept on their estates tor-

---

* Hume's Essays, Part II. Essay 11.

† Prof. W. A. Becker's Biblio. Sac., vol. ii. p. 571.

mentors by profession, for the purpose of punishing their slaves. Burying alive was sometimes resorted to; and crucifixion was frequently made the fate of a slave for trifling misconduct, or from mere caprice. They were slain as food for fishes; and the question often arose, whether, in a storm, a man should sacrifice a horse or a less valuable slave.*

It is for the infidel to show, when these were the prevailing views and sentiments on the subject of slavery throughout the world,—when in all the writings of ancient sages and moralists no other views are expressed,—when with the severest moralists of ancient times there is no denunciation of the system,—when there was nothing in the principles which they inculcated that would tend to subvert the institution of slavery or lead to emancipation,—how it happened that fishermen from Judea, uneducated men, gave utterance to the noble sentiments in the New Testament, and laid down principles utterly opposed to slavery, and that would, in their fair application, emancipate every slave on the face of the earth. Of this fact it is right that the friends of the Bible should be able to avail themselves; but of this fact they cannot avail themselves if it be maintained that the Bible is favourable to slavery, or if slavery is countenanced and sustained in the Christian church. This one thing is as certain as any thing can be:—that there are large—increasingly large—classes of men who never *can* be convinced that a book is a revelation from God which abets and upholds slavery, or which can be used as a defence of

* Wayland's Letters on Slavery, pp. 86, 87.

slavery as it exists in our land. We must either give up the point that the New Testament defends slavery, or we *must* give up a very large—and an increasingly large—portion of the people of this land to infidelity; for they neither can, nor will, nor ought to be convinced that a book that sanctions slavery is from God. I believe that this must and should be so; and that there are great principles in our nature, as God has made us, which can never be set aside by *any* authority of a pretended revelation; and that if a book professing to be a revelation from God by any fair interpretation defended slavery, or placed it on the same basis as the relation of husband and wife, parent and child, guardian and ward, such a book neither ought to be, nor could be, received by mankind as a divine revelation.

Hence it seems to me to be so important that the church should assume a just position on this subject, by detaching itself wholly from slavery, just as it detaches itself from piracy, intemperance, theft, licentiousness, and duelling. Let these things be or be not defended by the world; let them be or be not upheld by men who make no pretensions to religion; let the people of the world outside of the church judge of them as they please; but from each and all forms of oppression, and wrong, and cruelty, and fraud, let the church stand aloof, bearing a solemn testimony to mankind in regard to the evil of these things. On these points, and on all points of wrong, let the church place itself where it shall not be possible to mistake its position; where its example can never be plead in justification of these things; and where the infidel can never allege, in support of his own views, that the church of God, professing a belief in an inspired book, places itself in a position where the doctrines which it holds, and the sentiments which it aims to propagate, impinge on great principles of human nature, and make it impossible, if they are the fair teachings of that book, to receive it as a revelation from God.

It is impossible not to reflect on the noble position which the Christian church would occupy if the sentiments which have been advocated in this essay should become the practical sentiments of the church at large. Should such views prevail, what an example would it furnish to the world at large! Then the authority of the church could no more be urged in favour of a system which practically annuls the obligation of the marriage-vow, dissolves or ignores the authority of parents over their children, withholds from them the word of God, robs them of the avails of their labour, and subjects them to cruelties and wrongs for which by law they have no redress and of which they may not even complain. Then the attack on Christianity as upholding such a system would cease, and it could no more be alleged with any show of plausibility that the Bible justifies oppression and wrong. Then the infidel abolitionist could no more upbraid the church for maintaining sentiments which violate all the great and generous principles of our nature; and then he could no longer present himself—as he may do now, and actually does now—as holding sentiments and maintaining doctrines more in accordance with the great principles of humanity—more in accordance with what God has enstamped on man's heart—than are held by those who profess to receive the Bible as a revelation from God:—giving to infidelity, under the form of abolitionism, the advantage of being more in conformity with the laws of our being, and therefore with the laws of God, than the teachings of the Bible. Then the enemies of our country could no more revile the church for upholding a system which is becoming more and more offensive to mankind; for defending, in a land that is the boasted asylum of liberty, a system of oppression which is now without a parallel in the worst forms of government in the despotic systems of the Old World; and then the churches abroad would no more have occasion to remonstrate with the churches at home for contributing to uphold a system that violates all their notions of the gospel. Then the church of God would present an unbroken front in opposing a system which deprives three millions of human beings of every right with which their Creator has endowed them; effaces from those made in the image of God, as far as it can be done, every trace of that image; and treats as articles of barter and sale, trade and traffic, —as chattels and things,—those for whom the Redeemer shed his precious blood. God grant, in his infinite mercy, that the time may speedily come when some chief-justice shall utter, on the bench of the highest tribunal in the land, the noble sentiment of Mansfield:—'The air *of America* is too pure for a slave, and every man is free who breathes it;' and God grant, as preliminary to that, and as placing the church on the ground which at such a period it ought to occupy, that it may soon become a fact known to all men that among the ministers of religion in this land not one can be found who will be an apologist or an advocate for slavery; that from no ecclesiastical body shall an influence go forth to extend or perpetuate the system; that among all the ministers and members of the churches not one shall hold a fellow-man in bondage; and that no infidel, looking on this system of oppression, cruelty, and wrong, shall be able to say, on the authority of any minister of religion, any member of a Christian church, any expositor of the Bible, or any editor of a religious paper, that this system is sustained by what professes to be a revelation from God!

PHILADELPHIA, *October*, 1856.

THE END.

STEREOTYPED BY L. JOHNSON & CO.
PHILADELPHIA.

Rev. Albert Barnes' Books.

THE WAY OF SALVATION

Illustrated in a Series of Thirty-six Discourses. By the Rev. ALBERT BARNES. 1 vol. 12mo. Cloth, ... $1.00

CONTENTS:—The Bible—Obscurities of Divine Revelation—Claims of the Christian Religion—The Condition of Man not benefited by rejecting Christianity—The importance of Man—The Earth a place of Probation—Man on Probation—Necessity of accommodating ourselves to the Divine Government—The State in which the Gospel finds Man—What must I do to be saved?—Conviction of Sin—Struggles of a Convicted Sinner—A wounded Spirit—What will give permanent Peace?—The Mercy of God—The Atonement as fitted to give Peace—The Atonement as it removes the Obstacles in the way of Pardon—The Necessity of Regeneration—The Nature of Regeneration—Agency of the Spirit in Regeneration—The Nature of Repentance—The Relation of Repentance to pardon in the Christian System—Philosophical Necessity of Repentance—Foundation of the Command to Repent—Evidences of true Repentance—Faith a Condition of Salvation—Value and Importance of Faith—Faith as an Elementary Principle of Action—How shall Man be just with God?—Man cannot justify himself by Denying or Disproving the charge of Guilt—Man cannot justify himself by showing that his Conduct is right—Man cannot merit Salvation—What is meant by the merits of Christ—In what sense we are justified by the merits of Christ—The Influence of Faith in Justification—The Bearing and Importance of Justification by Faith.

"To the sinner, whether awakened or unawakened—to the penitent, whether seeking pardon or rejoicing in it—to the thoughtful, whether a believer or a sceptic—to the intelligent mind, of whatever class and under whatever circumstances, this treatise on the 'WAY OF SALVATION' may be heartily and hopefully recommended."—*E. Henderson, D. D.*, London.

"The volume cannot fail to benefit the Christian cause."—*Colonial Presbyterian.*

"In handling his weighty themes, Mr. Barnes employs a sinewy strength of argument, a striking originality of illustration, and a practical common sense, which need no enforcement from rhetorical common-places."—*N. Y. Tribune.*

"Characterized by clearness of statement, felicity of illustration, vigor of thought, and that quiet earnestness which gives a charm to every thing from the pen of Mr. Barnes."—*Independent.*

"As specimens of theological reasoning, of homiletic ability and completeness, and of practical religious feeling, we know of no writings of Mr. Barnes' superior. They are clear in thought, thorough in reasoning, and animated in style; and so impregnated with the personal experiences of the author, as to be deeply affecting in their earnestness and adaptedness."—*N. Y. Evangelist.*

SCRIPTURAL VIEWS OF SLAVERY.

An Inquiry into the Scriptural Views of Slavery. By Rev. ALBERT BARNES. 1 vol. 12mo. Cloth, ... $1.00

CONTENTS:—Introduction. Chap. 1.—Reasons why the Appeal on the Subject of Slavery should be made to the Bible. Chap. 2.—What Constitutes Slavery? Chap. 3.—Slavery in the Time of the Patriarchs. Chap. 4.—Slavery in Egypt. Chap. 5.—The Mosaic Institutions in relation to Servitude. Chap. 6.—Hebrew Servitude in the time of the Prophets. Chap. 7.—The relation of Christianity to Slavery.

"A calm, patient, reverential, and candid investigation of the teaching of Scripture on the subject of slavery."—*Religious Herald.*

"A dispassionate and thorough treatise upon the *Scriptural Views of Slavery.*"—*Independent.*

PRACTICAL SERMONS:

Designed for Vacant Congregations and Families. By Rev. ALBERT BARNES. 1 vol. 12mo. Cloth, ... $1.00

CONTENTS:—The Freeness of the Gospel—The Love of God in the Gift of a Saviour—Why will ye die?—The Deceitfulness of the Heart—Indecision in Religion—The Reason why men are not Christians—The Misery of forsaking God—God is worthy of Confidence—Repentance—Salvation Easy—The Principles upon which a Profession of Religion should be made (2 sermons)—Enemies of the Cross of Christ (3 sermons)—The Rule of Christianity in regard to Conformity to the World—The Blessings of a Benignant Spirit—Secret Prayer—The Sabbath—Secret Faults—Preparation to meet God—The Burden of Dumah—The Harvest Past.

"Ministers of the Gospel may derive many valuable suggestions from this book to aid them in their preparations for the pulpit; and Christians generally will find that a prayerful perusal of them is adapted to inform the judgment, and to improve the heart."—*Christian Visiter.*

THE GOSPELS: WITH MORAL REFLECTIONS ON EACH VERSE.

By PASQUIER QUESNEL. With an Introductory Essay, by the Rev. DANIEL WILSON, A. M., Vicar of Islington, [now Bishop of Calcutta.] Carefully revised by the Rev. HENRY A. BOARDMAN, D. D. Printed with bold type, on beautifully tinted and sized paper. 2 vols. 8vo. $4.

The following letters of commendation from eminent Clergymen, and brief extracts selected from numerous notices of the religious and secular press, are submitted, by the publishers, as evidence of the very high character of the work.

"We have no work of the same kind; we have nothing in practical divinity so sweet, so spiritual, so interior as to the real life of grace—so rich, so copious, so original. We have nothing that extols the grace of God, and abases and lowers man so entirely. We lessen not the value of our various admirable comments on the New Testament; they have each their particular excellencies. But none of them supersedes QUESNEL; none can supply that thorough insight into the world, the evil of sin, the life of faith and prayer, which he possesses."—*Bishop Wilson.*

"A repository of original, striking, spiritual Meditations, the absence of which could be supplied by no other work in our language."—*Dr. Boardman.*

(From the Right Rev. Alonzo Potter, D. D., Bishop of the Protestant Episcopal Church for the Diocese of Pennsylvania.)

Philadelphia, Oct. 31, 1855.

Messrs. Parry & McMillan,

Gentlemen—*Quesnel's Reflections* was an invaluable contribution to the sacred literature of the world in its original form. In this edition, prepared under the auspices of such names as Bishop Wilson and the Rev. Dr. Boardman, it will be still more useful for English and Protestant readers. It occupied a large part of the life of one of the most illustrious Jansenists of the 17th century; and to Ministers of the Gospel, and to private Christians of every name, it must always be an inexhaustible mine of interest and instruction. Your press could have rendered no better service to the public than by such an edition of such a work. I am, gentlemen, very truly, yours,

ALONZO POTTER.

(From Rev. William R. Williams, D. D., Pastor of Amity street Baptist Church, N. York.)

New York, 24th October, 1855.

Messrs. Parry & McMillan,

Gentlemen—I have for some years been almost daily in the use of Quesnel in the original French. It is blemished there with some Romanisms that are withdrawn in your revision. Bengel excels it in nice discrimination, and a most pregnant, epigrammatic brevity. With that exception, Quesnel seems to me to deserve rank *at the head of practical, devout, and spiritual expositions of the New Testament.* As revised, in your beautiful edition, its general circulation would, in the subscriber's judgment, be one of the richest boons that could be conferred on the various Evangelical churches of our country.

I am, gentlemen, yours, very resp'y,

WILLIAM R. WILLIAMS.

(From the Rev. Mr. Wylie, Pastor of First Reformed Presbyterian Church, Philadelphia.)

Messrs. Parry & McMillan,

Gentlemen—I rejoice to find that you have given to the American public so handsome an edition of Quesnel's Moral Reflections on the Gospels. There is a fulness, a freshness, a sweetness in this work which make it delightful reading, and now that it has passed under the revision of two such Editors as Bishop Wilson and Dr. Boardman, it may be considered perfectly free from any tincture of Romanism. I regard it as a most valuable addition to a library, and would commend it to the preacher, the Sabbath-school teacher, and the private Christian, as a most profitable and agreeable companion, in the study of the Gospels. I hope it may have such a circulation as will lead to the publication of his writings on the other parts of the New Testament. With great regard, truly yours,

T. W. J. WYLIE.

Philadelphia, Nov., 1855.

Messrs. Parry & M'Millan,

Gentlemen—You are very welcome to the use of my name as recommending the valuable and eminently spiritual work of "Quesnel on the Gospels," which you have just published.

CHAS. P McILVAINE.

Cincinnati, Nov. 27, 1855. *Bishop of the Prot. Ep. Ch. in Ohio.*

(From Rev. W. Adams, D. D., Pastor of Madison Square Presbyterian Church.)

New York City, 6th Nov., 1855.

Messrs. Parry & McMillan,

Gentlemen—I rejoice in the republication of *Quesnel on the Gospels.* It is the life-labor of a good and great man. We owe more to the Jansenists than has been acknowledged. Here and there may remain in Pascal, Thomas a'Kempis and Quesnel, Romish notions—flies in the ointment—which are easily separated from the fragrant mass. There is an uncommon richness, pith, and quaintness in the Reflections of Quesnel, which will secure for them that esteem they deserve, when they are better known. The excellent taste and judgment of the American Editor, are a pledge that every weed has been culled from this garden of spices. Very respectfully, your Obt. Servt.,

W. ADAMS.

(From the Rev. Dr. Alexander, Pastor of the Fifth Avenue and Nineteenth street Presbyterian Church, New York.)

New York, Oct. 24, 1855.

The work of Quesnel on the Gospels, is a series of Devotional Reflections, which has commanded the suffrages of Protestants. As corrected, it is, in my opinion, more full of holy suggestion, especially for Ministers of the Word, than any similar writing; indeed, it breathes the best spirit of Gerson, Pascal and Fenelon. But its chief glory is its condemnation by the famous Constitution UNIGENITUS, of Pope Clement the Eleventh. I rejoice in the republication of a book so precious.

JAMES W. ALEXANDER.

(From Thomas De Witt, D. D., of the Collegiate Reformed Dutch Church, New York.)

New York, 26th Oct., 1855.

I esteem the neat edition of "Quesnel's Moral Reflections on the Gospels," published by Parry & McMillan, under the revision of Dr. Boardman, highly valuable for profitable religious use. The Reflections are eminently judicious, and richly spiritual and practical. Few works of the kind are so well adapted for edification in the devout reading of the Gospels. The divine life in the soul is happily and strikingly delineated, and the practical bearing of the truth upon the discipline of the heart and regulation of the life, is most wisely and impressively borne home in these volumes. I sincerely hope that they may obtain an extensive patronage, and wide circulation in the different branches of the Christian church.

THOMAS DE WITT.

(From the Rev. J. P. Durbin, D. D., of the Methodist Episcopal Church, Philadelphia.)

Philadelphia, Oct., 1855.

Messrs. Parry & McMillan,

Gentlemen—Many years ago, when I first began to study the Bible, with aid from the writings of others, my attention was directed to the pious Quesnel, by the depth and truth of his Moral and Religious Reflections on the Gospels. Without endorsing his peculiar speculative opinions, which appear occasionally, I heartily commend his Notes or Reflections on the Gospels, verse by verse. They address themselves to the heart of the lay reader; and are fruitful aids to the minister in preparing for the pulpit.

J. P. DURBIN.

(From E. L. Cleaveland, D. D., of the Congregational Church, New Haven.)

The publication in this country of Quesnel's celebrated work on the Gospels, over whose truth-telling pages Rome has trembled and saints have rejoiced, is a long-needed and most valuable addition to our religious literature. I am glad that its full, sparkling current of original thought,—rich in all the graces of the Spirit,—is henceforth to water and fertilize the churches of our land.

E. L. CLEAVELAND.

New Haven, Nov. 20, 1855.

EXTRACTS FROM NOTICES OF THE PRESS.

"This world-renowned work, the richest product of Jansenist Theology, impressed with the imprimatur of the Pope's anathema, is now for the first time published in this country. * * * * It will be read in this country, as it has long been in Europe, by thousands to their spiritual edification."—*Biblical Repertory and Princeton Review.*

"We think that all good people, and clergymen especially, will greatly enjoy, and be largely profited by these 'Reflections.' They are not a comment on the Gospels, but each verse is followed by a few lines suggesting its spiritual richness and beauty, and often opening its religious sense with charming and surprising force. The volumes are admirably printed in large and fair type, and in excellent taste."—*Congregationalist.*

"We doubt not that ministers and private Christians will find these volumes to be a store-house of spiritual treasures."—*N. Y. Observer.*

"Quesnel has left nothing unwinnowed but the finest of the wheat."—*Nat. Intel.*

THE BOOK AND ITS STORY.

The Book and its Story; a Narrative for the Young on the occasion of the Jubilee of the British and Foreign Bible Society. By D. N. R. With an Introductory Preface by the Rev. T. PHILLIPS, Jubilee Secretary. Handsomely printed, in one volume, crown octavo, on fine paper, and illustrated with numerous wood cuts. Cloth, . $1.00

"The 'Story' of The Book, in all ages, countries, and languages, is told with simplicity and truthfulness. The work contains the 'Story' of the Bible from the first dawn of Revelation to the completion of the Sacred Canon, with the interesting tales of its translation and circulation, from the earliest efforts to the present time. To tell the Story of the Book in former days, a multitude of curious facts have been culled from works of difficult access; and its latter progress is illustrated by an abundant variety of statements drawn from numerous authentic sources."—*Preface.*

"This valuable work, containing the 'Story' of that wonderfully preserved book—the Bible—should be heartily welcomed by all the Christian families of this land. Interesting and instructive, it attracts the youth, and at the same time furnishes strong food for the man of reflection and mature years. We hope that the publishers will be more than remunerated for the introduction of such a work into the Christian literature of this land."—*Inquirer & Courier.*

"To the man who loves God's Word, and who is desirous of seeing it circulated in all the nations of our earth, this book is an inestimable treasure. It ought to be in every family and congregational library. Its perusal must profit every man who glances over its pages."—*Reform Banner.*

"One of the most important and valuable works we have ever commended. It possesses throughout a powerful interest."—*American Courier.*

"It places before us, in a most attractive form, the history of the Bible itself, and the countries connected with that history from the earliest date, blending with the statements details of a highly instructive character, well calculated to enlighten the mind, and to impress the heart with feelings of reverence for the 'Oracles of the Living God.' We strongly recommend the work as a most pleasing and instructive addition to the family library."—*Church Witness.*

"The work can scarcely fail to be received with as much favor in this country as in England, where it has gone through eleven editions in little longer than a year."—*Com. Advertiser.*

"This book will be sought by Christians of all denominations. It is indeed a most charming history of the Bible."—*Daily News.*

"Great pains seem to have been taken to render the varied contents of the volume as accurate as they are interesting."—*Sat. Eve. Post.*

"This book, we understand, has already passed through *nineteen* editions in England. It has now commenced its American career, and we think the firm of Messrs. Parry & McMillan has been particularly judicious in selecting a work of so much excellence, and which was so much needed to fill up the desideratum which was felt in religious and useful knowledge. Though the work was written professedly for the young, the old may be profited thereby; and no family should be without it."—*Rel. Intelligencer.*

"This is precisely such a book as should be found in every family. The wood cuts and illustrations are exceedingly valuable. The publishers display great taste in the getting up of the work."—*Pres. Banner.*

"A deeply interesting volume. We shall rejoice to know that a copy of this choice volume is finding its way to every family in the land."—*Christian Visitor.*

"We know of no book for general readers that covers the same ground. It well deserves the popularity it has attained."—*Journal & Advocate.*

"The writer has obviously brought to his task large information and an earnest spirit; and he has imparted these in such a way to his pages as to make them both instructive and attractive."—*North American.*

"It is no disparagement to say that the Story of 'THE BOOK' enhances its interest. The dealings of Providence in its preservation and spread, put on it a value even beyond what is intrinsic. We heartily recommend this volume as a stimulant to the study of the Bible."—*N. O. Chris. Adv.*

"It is a book of remarkable value; has specimens of the text of nearly all the most ancient manuscript copies of the Holy Writings in various languages, and a view of the first public reading of the Scriptures in the Crypt of St. Paul's, London, in the year 1541."—*Concordia Intelligencer*

"It contains an exceedingly interesting account of the Bible in past ages, giving sketches of the condition of the nations of former times, who were destitute of the light of divine revelation, relating briefly the history of the Old and New Testament Scriptures, and the various translations of them in ancient and modern languages. * * * Altogether the book is an excellent one, and is calculated to increase our estimate of the value of the Scriptures, and our interest in their circulation."—*Banner of the Covenant.*

The Six Days of Creation.

By W. G. Rhind. A Series of affectionate Letters from a Father to his Children, developing the progressive advances of Creation during the Six Days: in which the Natural History of Animals, Plants, Minerals, Celestial Objects, etc., and their uses and relations to man, are treated with particular reference to the illustration of Scriptural truth. A highly interesting work. From the last London edition. With numerous illustrations. 1 vol. crown 8vo. Cloth, - $1.00

"An elegant manual for the young; far superior to any of the season, and to the large majority that we have seen at any time. We have read it with unalloyed satisfaction. It combines the very best qualities of a youthful instructor. and is a storehouse of the most useful information. * * * * We earnestly recommend this book to parents. as one of the most charming and beneficial presents they can make to their children. The author has the interest of the rising generation deeply at heart, and the ability to prove a blessing to it."—*Methodist Quarterly Review.*

"We can recommend it as an excellent family book, and the more there are like it the better. * * * The work abounds with graphic pictorial illustrations, and can scarcely fail to interest, and instruct, and sharpen the appetite for scriptural truth."—*Christian Intelligencer.*

"The work is beautifully brought out by the American publishers, having the advantage over the English edition of a great many beautiful cuts of the various objects of natural history, whilst all the engravings of that edition are accurately reproduced in this. It will be found to be an excellent aid to parents."—*Watchman and Observer.*

"We can safely say that in the same space in any work we have not met with so much substantial information, conveyed in such an attractive way. There are six steel plates illustrative of the appearance of our planet at the close of each of the six days' work, with a vast number of cuts presenting the images of the various animals, birds, &c., and which will be very attractive to young readers. * * * We would most earnestly recommend it to the notice of managers of congregational libraries and parents, as eminently suggestive and illustrative of lessons which should be impressed upon the minds of the young. * * * The work is alike admirable in design and execution. We wish it the widest possible circulation."—*Colonial Presbyterian.*

"An admirable book for family instruction."—*N. Orleans Picayune.*

"A more valuable or delightful volume than this cannot be put into the hands of youth. * * * The style of this excellent book is extremely pleasing, and its whole tone of a high order of genuine but simple piety. * * * We cordially commend it to the patronage of all parents."—*St. John Observer.*

"It ought to find a ready access to the families of all the lovers of an evangelical literature."—*Christian Visiter.*

"The amount of useful information this book contains respecting the natural history of the earth and the living creatures which inhabit it, is immense. But its peculiar merit consists in its familiarising the reader with the idea of the Creating Power. The young person who uses this book in order to obtain a knowledge of the works of creation, will ever after associate with natural objects the Author of nature. In an age when so many evil influences are acting upon the opening minds of the young, this *good influence* can hardly be overestimated."—*North American.*

"This is a most elegant and excellent book. It is not a discussion of Geological theories, but a grouping of facts in natural science—facts in Geology, Mineralogy, Natural History, Botany, &c. * * * It is a good 'Natural Theology' for children. where they can learn at the same time what kind of a world they live in, and who made it."—*Central Chris. Herald.*

"We can recommend the work to parents as a valuable present to families."—*St. Louis Intelligencer.*

"A book which every Christian parent should place in the hands of his children."—*Savannah Journal and Courier.*

"A book, in all respects, of excellent tendency."—*Puritan Recorder.*

"We deem it a duty to call the attention of parents and teachers to this work, in which the elements of Geology, Astronomy, Natural Philosophy, Zoology, and other sciences, are set forth with much clearness. * * * It is important when so many skeptical books are put in circulation, that the young should be early convinced that true science is in harmony with Revelation."—*N. Y. Com. Advertiser.*

"Not a geological, but a practically religious book, very beautifully got up. It is quite refreshing to peruse a devotional and well-written volume on this theme, that has been so long the prey of science, that the religion of it has been regarded as a secondary matter. We cordially commend this beautiful book to all readers, especially the young."—*N. Y. Obs.*

"It is just such a publication as parents will wish to have by them when they seek to teach their children the meaning of the sacred volume it illustrates."—*Boston Atlas.*

"A thoroughly evangelical spirit pervades the volume, adapting it to impress the heart, as well as inform the understanding."—*Presbyterian.*

The Ocean.

By P. H. Gosse, author of "An Introduction to Geology," "The Canadian Naturalist," etc. With fifty-two illustrations. From the last London edition. 1 vol. 12mo. Cloth, ... $1.00

Contents:—Introduction.—1. The Shores of Britain.—2. Same subject continued.—3. The Arctic Seas.—4. The Atlantic Ocean.—5. The Pacific Ocean.—6. Same subject continued. —7. The Indian Ocean.

In the above work, the author has described, with minuteness of detail, a few of the many objects of interest more or less directly connected with the Sea, and especially has he endeavored to lead youthful readers to associate with the phenomena of nature, habitual thoughts of God. A subject so vast as the Ocean might be viewed in a variety of aspects, all of them more or less instructive. The one which has been chosen is that in which it presents itself to the mind of a naturalist, desirous of viewing the Almighty Creator in His works. The selections are made chiefly from Marine Botany, Zoology, Meterology, the Fisheries, the varying aspects of Island and Coast Scenery, Incidents of Navigation, Atmospheric Phenomena, &c., arranged in the order of geographical distribution, as they might be supposed to present themselves to an observant voyager.

"We know of no work better calculated to lead the mind to associate with the various phenomena of nature, habitual thoughts of God, and an awe-inspiring admiration of His manifold works and power."—*Sinclair's Monthly Circular.*

"A very charming book, and one that every parent may be glad to put into the hands of his children, sure that they will be benefited and amused by it; and we fancy there are few parents who might not learn themselves something from its perusal."—*Montreal Gazette.*

"This book is full of instructive and entertaining information. * * * One might go to sea for years and not learn as much about the Ocean as he can gather from a few hours' study of this volume. Its moral and religious instruction also forms one of its chief features."—*N. Y. Observer.*

"A more instructive book cannot be placed in the hands of young people."—*Providence Journal.*

"We take pleasure in recommending this charming volume as a work which blends singularly and felicitously a fund of instruction with the highest interest."—*N. Orleans Bee.*

"Full of interest and instruction."—*N. Y. Christian Adv. and Journal.*

"The religious tone of the volume is pure, and the youthful heart, in tracing Mr. Gosse's pages, can scarcely refrain from associating God with the works of His hand."—*Western Christian Advocate.*

"Both in respect to illustrations and style, it deserves a place in every home, as well as in every lyceum library."—*Episcopal Recorder.*

"The author is perfectly at home in the department of natural science to which his book relates; and he has succeeded admirably in making the sea a witness for the benevolence and wisdom of God. Though the work seems primarily intended as a contribution to popular science, the devout mind will hardly fail to find in it much valuable material for religious contemplation."—*Puritan Recorder.*

"The volume is adapted to awaken a fresh sense of the vast resources of nature, and to inspire a feeling of religious awe, in the contemplation of the perpetual miracles of creation."—*N. Y. Tribune.*

"The book is a good one to buy for family reading, and would by no means be out of place, in our opinion, in the libraries of our Sunday Schools."—*Congregationalist.*

"The author occupies a high place among the naturalists of the day, and his book bears evidence of the extent and accuracy of his attainments, while he every where shows a most delightful spirit of piety and a habit of looking up from nature to nature's God."—*Banner and Advocate*

"A work of deep interest and full of instruction."—*Am. and Com. Advertiser.*

"A delightful volume of popular science, embracing every variety of information on marine subjects"—*N. Y. Com. Adv.*

"We are pleased with both the design and execution of this book. * * * From among the various sea formations and inhabitants the author has made a judicious selection, and teaches lessons which are calculated at once to instruct the understanding and improve the heart."—*Presbyterian.*

"Fascinating as a romance, reliable as history, and sterling as a moral essay."—*Am. Courier.*

"Taking the great oceans one by one, it makes you intimate with their geography, their winds, their tides, their zoology, and in short with more marvels than are dreamed of by the myriads of careless passengers whom the rushing steamer whirls from port to port."—*N. Y. Albion.*

SERMONS, DOCTRINAL AND PRACTICAL.

By the Rev. WILLIAM ARCHER BUTLER, A. M., late Professor of Moral Philosophy in the University of Dublin. Edited by the very Rev. THOMAS WOODWARD, A. M., Dean of Down. First Series. From the Third London edition. 1 vol. crown 8vo. Cloth, . . . $1.25

CONTENTS:—Uncertainty of Christ's Coming—The Incarnation—Daily Self-denial of Christ—Crucifying the Son of God afresh—The Power of the Resurrection—The Trinity disclosed in the Structure of St. John's Writings—Meetness for the Inheritance of the Saints in Light—Occasional mysteriousness of Christ's Teaching—Christ our Life—Self-delusion as to our real state before God—The Eternal Life of Christ in Heaven—The Canaanite Woman a type of the Gentile Church—The Faith of Man and the Faithfulness of God—The Wedding Garment—Christ sought and found in the Old Testament Scriptures—Human Affections raised, not destroyed, by the Gospel—The Rest of the People of God—Christ the Treasury of Wisdom and Knowledge—The Divinity of our Priest, Prophet and King—Expediency of Christ's Invisibility—The Invisible Government of Christ through His Spirit—Chris 's Departure the Condition of the Spirit's Advent—The Faith that cometh by Hearing—The Christian's Walk in Light and Love—Primitive Church Principles not inconsistent with Universal Christian Sympathy.

"Present a richer combination of the qualities for Sermons of the first class than any we have met with in any living writer."—*British Quarterly.*

"One destined, if we mistake not, to take the highest place among the writers of our English tongue."—*North British Review*, Feb. 1856.

"May justly take rank with the first writings in our language."—*Theologian.*

"An eminent divine and a profound thinker."—*English Review.*

"Poet, orator, metaphysician, theologian."—*Dublin University Magazine.*

"A burning and a shining light."—*Bishop of Exeter.*

"A man of whom, bo h as regards his life and his remarkable powers, his church may justly be proud."—*Guardian.*

"Entitled to stand in the front rank, not merely of ministers of the Irish church, but of the wisest and best teachers of all denominations."—*Wesleyan Magazine.*

"Discrimination and earnestness, beauty and power, a truly philosophical spirit."—*British Quarterly.*

MORNINGS WITH JESUS.

A series of Devotional Readings for the Closet and the Family for every day in the year, carefully prepared from notes of sermons preached by the late Rev. Wm. Jay, of Bath. 1 vol. crown 8vo. Cloth, gilt, $1.25

"The Rev. Wm. Jay was the clergyman whom John Foster, the celebrated essayist, entitled 'the prince of preachers.' Judging from this volume, the very skeleton of his discourse has more energy than the entire body of some men's pulpit oratory."—*Com. Adv.*

"These Readings breathe a spirit of genuine piety, and their tone is catholic and healthful."—*Evening Argus.*

"Charmingly adapted to private and family reading. The Sunday School teacher will find it an invaluable assistant."—*City Item.*

"This well printed volume contains numerous expositions of the sacred scriptures, marked by the originality and naturalness of manner, the perspicuity and impressiveness of style, the evangelical and experimental savour. the fullness and felicity of illustration, which were characteristic of the discourses of their pious and eloquent author. Clearness of thought, vigor of expression, boldness in the utterance of truth, and earnestness both of persuasion and denunciation, are traits in which they eminently excel."—*N. Am.*

"The brief meditations composing the volume are pervaded with some of the best characteristics of Mr. Jay's style, and will not disappoint the devout reader."—*Presbyterian.*

"These meditations are, like everything from the pen, or the lips, of William Jay, practical, evangelical, apt, and often strikingly beautiful. * * * * Full of pious and excellent thought, and well fitted to be read in connection with the devotions of either the family or the closet."—*Puritan Recorder.*

"There is a peculiar freshness about these pages which gives them a charm superior to almost any other of the productions of Mr. Jay."—*N. Y. Observer.*

"Christians, who know the worth of evangelical truth, will value it as a volume worthy of being employed to aid their private and family devotions; and, whether beginning the Christian life, or more advanced in the experience of it, will read it with profit and pleasure."—*Church Witness.*

"One great charm that pervades these pages is, that they range through every department of human experience, and show that the Spirit has his appropriate teachings for every condition. They are also eminently fitted to cherish a devotional spirit."—*Dr. Sprague.*

EVENINGS WITH THE PROPHETS:

A Series of Memoirs and Meditations. By REV. A. MORTON BROWN, LL. D., Cheltenham. 1 vol. crown 8vo., ... $1.00

"This is a volume of high merit both as an elucidation and a defence of the Scriptures. It is not addressed to the select and lettered few; but to the great multitude, who are capable of appreciating the results of learning, and are anxious to obtain clear and connected views of the lives, characters, and writings of holy men of God, who spake as they were moved by the Holy Ghost. It is emphatically a book for the people, and as such it cannot fail to be attended with results happy, permanent, and extensive. No mind but one replete with knowledge, and familiar with the entire range of sacred literature, could have produced it; and yet the whole is pervaded by a freshness and a lucid simplicity that must invest it with high interest to all readers. There is nothing to be seen of the dry elaboration of criticism, or of the formality and stiffness of mere comment. Each chapter and section flow on clear, comprehensive, full, presenting the results rather than the process of criticism and learned investigation. And hence, while the volume will be warmly approved by scholars and divines. who are already acquainted with the questions discussed, it will be especially welcomed by the great body of the thoughtful and inquiring, who, without minute acquaintance with the literature of Biblical investigation and prophetic studies, are anxious to arrive at satisfactory views of the Bible as a whole. To the young, who are entering on an earnest examination of the Scriptures, in order to the attainment of clear conceptions of the harmony of divine truth; and to those of riper years, who are desirous of having their knowledge amplified or confirmed, it will prove an invaluable boon.

"* * * * * The full light of patient inquiry and ample knowledge shines on every topic of importance connected with the life, and labors, and times of the long train of prophets that pass in review, so that the reader finds himself, not merely looking on a vivid and life-like picture of gifted and inspired men, but surrounded with the circumstances and scenes through which they passed. The chapters resemble great historic paintings; each prophet stands as the centre, and around him gather the pomp and circumstance, and grandeur and desolation of ancient monarchies, the shadows of Israel's doom, and the rising splendors of Messiah's kingdom.

"* * * * As far as extensive knowledge and earnestness of purpose, combined with great ease and felicity in delineating characters and events, serve to throw interest around the grandest themes that can occupy the human mind, Dr. Brown's labors have, we think, been eminently successful. Readers, who have already accurate and comprehensive views of the various subjects discussed, will be gratified with the clearness and force with which they are handled; and many, whose notions of the sacred volume have been disjointed and fragmentary, will rise from the perusal of this book with conceptions of its unity which will excite their grateful and admiring wonder, and although not formally an argument for the divine authority of the Scriptures, it cannot be read without furnishing to all thinking minds attestations of the divinity of the Bible.

"* * * * The style in which the volume is written is easy, fresh, and varied, not unfrequently rising into great force and beauty. There are many examples of happy antitheses, and not a few gem-like passages of aphoristic wisdom. Sometimes there is an element of the dramatic running through Dr. Brown's sketches, and occasionally there are eloquent outbursts of indignant invective against tyranny and oppression. Throughout, indeed, the variety, spirit, and naturalness of the style are such that the reader glides along the pages with an ease that prevents all disturbance of thought, and secures an im mediate apprehension of the subject.

"We warmly commend the book to all classes of our readers, assured that its perusal cannot fail to yield them both pleasure and profit."—*London Evnagelical Magazine.*

HOWARD GREY: A STORY FOR BOYS.

By a young Lady of Philadelphia. 18mo., fine paper, pp. 231, cloth, $0.50

"A well-expressed book, pure in sentiment, wise in analysis and apprehension of character; and, in a genuine sense, moral and religious in influence."—*Bizarre.*

"An interesting little work."—*N. O. Delta.*

"Calculated to stimulate boys to earnest exertion."—*Watchman and Observer.*

"We seldom meet with a little story so carefully and powerfully written as this is. *Howard Grey* will be likely to make a deep impression for good upon the minds of the young readers to whom it is given. It will encourage them to perseverance in the path of duty, and patience under suffering and wrong."—*N. Y. Com. Advertiser.*

"We hope that the success of the author of Howard Grey may be such as to encourage her to often repeat her endeavours to amuse and instruct her young friends, both at home and abroad, by the publication of many more just such stories for boys."—*Boston Atlas.*

Russell's (Lady Rachel) Letters.

The Letters of Rachel, Lady Russell. New edition. Containing many Letters never before published. Complete in one handsome volume, 12mo., ... $1.25

"That sweet saint, that sate by
Russell's side—under the judgment seat."

"The volume now before us is one of the handsomest standard volumes of the season. It contains not only the letters that appeared in the first edition, but many others, written during the period of her happy wedded life, and that famous letter to her children, written on the anniversary of her husband's decease. It also embraces the copious notes by Miss Berry, and Mr. Martin. the librarian of Woburn Abbey."—*Boston Morning Post.*

"Lady Rachel Russell was the wife of the noble and unfortunate Lord William Russell, the compatriot of Algernon Sidney, and other illustrious asserters of English liberty in the seventeenth century. Her letters have passed through numerous editions in England, and have been long considered models of epistolary style. They are full of tender sentiment, and relate to matters of the most touching interest."—*Commercial Advertiser.*

"The Letters of Lady Russell contain but one topic and one resource—that topic the judicial murder of her husband—that resource the strength of a soul sustained by all the fortitude of a heroine, and chastened by all the piety of a saint."—*Buffalo Daily Courier.*

"The one great theme which these letters illustrate, was the judicial murder of Lord William Russell by Charles II. They reveal the soul of a heroine, and the piety of one taught in the school of Christ, and chastened by affliction to bear with pious resignation the severest trials, in obedience to the Divine will. These letters will be read with deep interest in connection with the history of England during the reign of Charles II."—*Christian Observer.*

"Lady Russell was a woman of pure spirit, unaffected piety, warm heart, tried virtues, and excellent understanding. Her letters have been often reprinted, and their merits have so long been familiar to the public that we need only call attention to some of the points in which this new and beautiful edition, by Messrs. Parry & M'Millan, surpasses any hitherto presented to the world."—*Banner of the Cross.*

"The appearance of a volume like the present. is among the rarest of *benefactions* conferred upon the public. For it offers to our view one of those noble and sublime specimens of our common humanity, whose thoughts and deeds 'enrich the blood of the world.' As a source of inspiration, of solace, and sustaining energy, it were impossible to estimate the influence exerted by a character like Lady Russell's, on all coming within its sphere. * * * The tragic history of her husband is, probably, as familiar to most, as her own. That most blameless of statesmen, Lord Somers, declared Lord Russell to have been '*murdered*' by the infamous pair, Charles II. and his brother James. How *devotedly attached* were the wife and husband. and how happy in this attachment, will abundantly appear from this volume; as will also the admirable conduct of Lady Russell during the trial and last days of her lord, and the *forty years* of widowhood that followed."—*Bizarre.*

"This is a very beautiful edition of the celebrated Letters of Lady Russell, and its value is enhanced by the copious foot notes which explain every allusion of a personal, historical, political or private nature in the letters, which might be unintelligible to common readers. The libertine, Charles II., and the Popish bigot James II., in their efforts to establish arbitrary power, had to trample out the lights of their day, that shone out and pointed the way to liberty. Amid these luminaries, Sydney and Russell shone as stars of the first magnitude, and both were murdered. Still their light continued to shine. The Revolution came, and Popery was defeated."—*Presbyterian Banner.*

Salomon's Sermons.

Twelve Sermons delivered in the New Temple of the Israelites at Hamburg. By Gotthold Salomon. Translated from the German by Anna Maria Goldsmid, ... $1.00

The Honey Bee: its Natural History, Physiology and Management.

By Edward Bevan. With 35 Engravings on Wood. 1 vol. Paper, $0.31

Poems.

By Louisa S. McCord. 1 vol. 12mo. Cloth, ... $0.75

A Survey of the Literature of the United States,

BY RUFUS WILMOT GRISWOLD.

I. THE POETS AND POETRY OF AMERICA.
II. THE FEMALE POETS OF AMERICA.
III. THE PROSE WRITERS OF AMERICA.

POETS AND POETRY OF AMERICA.

The Poets and Poetry of America; embracing Selections from the Poetical Literature of the United States, from the time of the Revolution. With a Preliminary Essay on the Progress and Condition of Poetry in this country—and Biographical and Critical Notices of the most eminent Poets. By RUFUS W. GRISWOLD. New edition; copiously illustrated with Portraits, from original designs, on steel; revised, enlarged, and brought down to the present time. 1 vol. 8vo. Cloth, . $3 00

Cloth extra, gilt edges, ... 3.50

Calf backs, Marbled Edges, ... 4.00

Turkey morocco, extra, ... 5.00

"A work entirely without a rival in its department, and for which there has for years existed a marked and increased necessity."—*National Intelligencer.*

"The best collection of American poetry that has been made."—*N. Y. Evening Post.*

"The editor, the Rev. R. W. Griswold, has culled from the wide field of American poetic literature, many of its rarest intellectual gems. The volume extends to 468 pages, is beautifully embellished, and cannot but prove an acceptable addition to every public and private library."—*Post.*

"It embodies in its pages much that is chaste, and fraught with the fire of true genius; is, emphatically, an American work, and is not a little creditable to our literature."—*Inquirer.*

"Mr. G. has done a service to our literature, which eminently entitles him to the regard and favour of a discerning and impartial public."—*National Intelligencer.*

"The whole volume is got up in a manner to do credit to the American poets, and to show that they are held in estimation."—*U. S. Gazette.*

"No better selection from the poetry of our native bards has ever been made, and no person could do better with the materials than Mr. Griswold has done."—*Boston Traveller.*

"It is performing a valuable service when a man of taste and information makes a suitable, well-assorted selection, and guides the friend of Poetry in his rambles through those groves from which he might otherwise be deterred by their immensity. Such service has been rendered by Mr. Griswold in his 'Poets and Poetry of America."—*Baron Frederick Von Raumer*, of Prussia.

"We doubt whether there is another man in America who could have been found to devote so much industry, not to say drudgery, as was called for in such an undertaking. Sure we are that no such man could have been found who would have done it so well."—*N. Y. Courier and Enquirer.*

"The editor has executed his task with industry, skill, and taste. No man in this country is probably so familiar with this branch of American literature, not only in regard to its most ancient, but most obscure authors."—*N. Y. Evening Post.*

"No collection of American poetry at all comparable to it in extent, completeness, or general merit, has ever been issued."—*Albany Evening Journal.*

"Mr. Griswold has succeeded as well in his book as the nature of the case admitted; his patient research and general correctness of taste are worthy of praise; his difficulties and temptations would have extenuated far graver errors than he has committed, and his volume well deserves the approbation it has received."—*North Am. Review (by E. P. Whipple).*

"We must not forget to thank Mr. Griswold for his good taste and good feeling. It would be difficult to overpraise either."—*London Examiner.*

"We think in this beautiful volume the reader will find nearly all that is worth reading in American poetry."—*Boston Morning Post.*

"Mr. Griswold's work is honorable to the character and genius of the American people." —*Thos. Campbell. author of "The Pleasures of Hope."*

"The critical and biographical notes are brief, but discriminative and elegant."—*Bishop Potter's "Hand-Book for Readers."*

The Female Poets of America.

By Rufus Wilmot Griswold. Illustrated with Portraits from original artists. New edition; revised, enlarged, and brought down to the present time. 1 vol. 8vo. Cloth, ... $3.00
Cloth extra, gilt edge, ... 3.50
Calf backs and corners, Marbled Edges, ... 4.00
Morocco extra, ... 5.00

"Very rare, and very opposite, and very high abilities are required for that circumnavigation of the whole continent of literature—that exploration of every bay, and river, and inland lake, with all their islands—that picturesque representation of every peculiarity of the subjects of research, sketchy yet faithful, spirited yet minute—and, above all, that grouping of the whole in one historical picture of national genius, which are demanded by the enterprise which Dr. Griswold has essayed, and which he has so successfully accomplished by a combination of knowledge and skill as uncommon as it is delightful. His biographical narratives display a great deal of spirit and tact. His criticisms exhibit a thorough familiarity with the writings which he reviews, and are animated with sensibilities and perceptions kindred in their delicacy and ardor with that inspiration from which the verses themselves have flowed. They are searching, truthful, comprehensive, and candid in their character, and always graceful and elegant in style."—*New York Tribune.*

"Dr. Griswold has performed the duties of his undertaking with a diligence, a taste, and a discrimination which we doubt whether any other man in this country could have equalled. The selections are copious and judicious, and the criticisms upon them are delicate and just. A great deal of trouble has obviously been taken to obtain materials for the work, and to bring together accurate information in regard to the authors. A very large portion of the poems have been given to the editor expressly for this collection. The work has, therefore, to a great extent, the value of an original production, by the combined efforts of our female poets."—*Morris and Willis's Home Journal.*

Prose Writers of America.

The Prose Writers of America. With a Survey of the Intellectual History, Condition, and Prospects of the Country. By Rufus Wilmot Griswold. Illustrated with Portraits from original artists. New edition. Complete in one volume, 8vo. Cloth, ... $3.00
Cloth, extra, gilt edges, ... 3.50
Calf backs, Marbled Edges, ... 4.00
Turkey morocco, extra, ... 5.00

"We deem this book by all odds the best of its kind that has ever been issued."—*N. Y. Courier & Inquirer.*

"The extracts with which it is illustrated, compose a mass of the finest passages in American literature, and are of a character which will secure for the volume a place on the book table of every man or woman of literary taste. The portraits, of which there are nine, are engraved in a very beautiful manner. 'It is not only an admirable survey of our literature, but a very interesting and important addition to it.'"—*Christian Observer.*

"It is a work of great research, and the task must have required an immensity of toil to draw from the mass of publication that which is most likely to interest the public, and to afford a perfect view of the peculiar powers of the writer."—*Neal's Gazette.*

"Mr. Griswold's book has been executed honestly, ably, and well, and is a valuable contribution to the literature of the country."—*Knickerbocker.*

"It is a faithful view of our best prose writers and their productions."—*Boston Atlas.*

"The book is valuable and very interesting; the biographies are well written, and the criticisms are in the main impartial. It is just the kind of book which the general reader will like to possess, and will afford pleasant reading for many a leisure half hour."—*N. Y. Com. Advertiser.*

"Dr. Griswold has performed his task as well as any man in the country would have done it. He has done American literature and American readers a service for which we thank him heartily. The book deserves, and we think will command general attention and approval."—*N. Y. Tribune.*

"We commend 'The Prose Writers of America' to a wide national acceptance; with the especial advice to the reader, not to overlook the excellent introductory 'Essay on the Intellectual History, Condition and Prospects of the Country,' which contains many noteworthy suggestions and much valuable information."—*Knickerbocker.*

LECTURES ON ENGLISH HISTORY,

As Illustrated by Shakspeare's Chronicle Plays, and on Tragic Poetry. By HENRY REED. Edited by his brother, WILLIAM B. REED. 1 vol. 12mo. $1.25

Messrs. Parry & M'Millan,

Gentlemen—Mr. Henry Reed's *Lectures on English Literature* and *English History* are works of great merit and rare beauty: indicating high powers of intellect, uncommon reading and research in the History and Literature of England, and a faculty, quite unique, of throwing around that which is didactic and instructive, a charm and interest due to the author himself.

I have recommended them in unqualified terms to such of my students as are sufficiently advanced to appreciate their merits; and I wish for them—what I am sure they are now attaining—a complete success, and a perusal wherever the English language is studied.

I am, gentlemen, most resp'y,

HY. COPPÉE,

University, January 29, 1856. Prof. Eng. Literature in the University of Penn'a.

"The student of Shakspeare will find many admirable suggestions in the critical analyses of the volume, nor will he ever fail to be gratified with the elevation of taste and beauty of language with which they are put forth."—*N. Y. Tribune.*

"We are commonly so much impressed by the merits of Shakspeare's more imaginative plays, that we are apt to lose sight of the greatness of this historical series; and it is only when they are brought together as a unity—as in these Lectures of Professor Reed—that we feel how wonderful they are. It is needless for us to add, that in his generalizations and criticisms, Prof. Reed evinces careful historical reading, fine taste, a noble and sweet humanity, and an ardent love of his topics."—*Putnam's Magazine.*

"In this posthumous volume by the late lamented Professor Reed, we have another evidence of the delicacy of his taste, his various and elegant culture, and his cordial appreciation of the great master-pieces of English literature."—*Harper's Magazine.*

"The work is no ephemeral production, but will take its place in standard literature as one of elegant and philosophical criticism."—*Dollar Newspaper.*

"The pure, transparent taste of Mr. Reed eminently qualified him for an exponent of the genius of Shakspeare. Among the myriad commentators who have attempted to elucidate the great poet's text, a more reverential and appreciative admirer, or one who has more entirely imbibed the spirit of the master-mind, is not to be found."—*Detroit Free Press.*

"Scarcely any writer of modern times on English Literature has so won our confidence and affection as Henry Reed. * * * Taking one of Shakspeare's plays as a text, he gathers up all the historic data which are needful to its illustration and confirmation; and thus employs the imagination of the great dramatist to illuminate and give distinctness to the historical period to which it refers; while he makes history, in its turn, reflect the beauty and truthfulness of the play; a plan alike novel and delightful."—*Boston Traveller.*

"Beginning with the dim legendary period on which Lear and Cymbeline shed a few rays of light, Mr. Reed, in these exquisite essays—for such, rather than lectures, they are—traces the varied course of English history down to the verge of the Poet's own day—the reign of Henry the Eighth and the birth of Elizabeth; and it is wonderful to be made to understand, by the continuity of such a mode of illustration, how complete the course is. Marlborough's confession of ignorance was not so great as one is apt to think, when he said that all he knew of English history he learned from Shakspeare's plays; and Mr. Reed shows us now how complete, and thorough, and accurate, the Poet's knowledge was. There is throughout a happy blending of criticism and history, and withal, in perhaps a greater degree than in Mr. Reed's former volume, that transparency of style which reveals in every page the pure and gentle character, the strong intelligence and high morality, of the author. No one that begins this little book will lay it down till it is finished. It is, too, suited to all tastes and all ages."—*North American.*

"Professor Reed has gained a transatlantic reputation of which any one might be proud; and it is enough for the work before us to say that it will add in a high degree to that reputation. * * * * These Lectures require no praise. No one can read them without adding materially to his stock of information, or without being impressed by the judicious relation of facts, the taste in illustration, or the purity of language everywhere displayed."—*Philad'a Evening Bulletin.*

"These Lectures show a knowledge not only of the text of England's greatest bard, but a deep and critical examination of their suggestions, and we believe will be found to be of inestimable value, as commentaries upon the genius of him who has long puzzled the acumen of scholars, and given food for thought to the great minds of every age. That they are valuable additions to the historical literature of our country, no one who knows Professor Reed's ability can for a moment doubt. * * * * For the collection of his works we are indebted to the affectionate regard of his brother, William B. Reed, Esq.; and we cannot take leave of the volume without expressing our satisfaction with the manner in which that gentleman has executed the task."—*Argus.*

REED'S LECTURES ON ENGLISH LITERATURE.

Lectures on English Literature, delivered in the Chapel Hall of the University of Pennsylvania, by Professor HENRY REED. With a Portrait. Edited by his brother, WILLIAM B. REED. 1 vol. 12mo. Cloth $1.25

"The sound and discriminating criticism with which this work abounds, will render it an acknowledged classic, both in Europe and America. It is the most important addition to critical literature which this country has produced. * * * We regard it as of inestimable value as aid in the higher walks of education. Our college students, and the young ladies in what are called 'finishing schools,' have had, hitherto, no reliable guide in the choice of their reading; no good text-book of English belles-lettres. This deficiency is now supplied, and we especially commend the 'Lectures on English Literature' to the notice of college professors, and the teachers of all the higher kinds of schools. * * * So important an acquisition should by no means be neglected.—*North American.*

"The book is in every way a most creditable contribution to the Library of Critical Literature."—*London Leader.*

"These lectures bear the marks of ripe scholarship, and an accomplished mind."—*Presbyterian.*

"We have examined this volume with that interest with which one would open a box of jewels, and examine, one by one, the specimens rich and rare. And when you add to this, the sad thought that the one who gathered such a collection of the solid, beautiful and costly in literature, went down with the three hundred who disappeared with the *Arctic* beneath the waves of the Atlantic, the interest increases to a tearful intensity, and you drink in the words of wisdom of the ocean-buried, as though they were baptized in a new inspiration."—*American Spectator.*

"The Lectures are of the highest order, both in scholarship, sound sense, and gracefulness of style, and show a thorough mastery of his subject that only a familiar acquaintance with the original sources could have given. There is also a moral purity and a Christian spirit running through them that is peculiarly pleasing."—*Watchman and Observer.*

"One of the greatest merits of these Lectures is their entire freedom from an affectedly profound philosophy; from an appearance of that German transcendentalism which soars so high as to reach beyond all real comprehension, and which penetrates to depths that are unfathomable, that analyses until nought remains, and that vanishes from all intelligence in an entangled forest of woodland. A genial spirit of healthy criticism pervades the work, which displays the purity and elvated tone of the lamented author."—*Presbyterian Banner.*

"* * * * If anything could bring consolation to the friends of Professor Reed for his untimely loss, it is that he left his MSS. in such a complete and scholar-like preparation that the public will receive them as a national benefit. * * * * The third lecture of the volume on the English language, is in itself a monument of the varied and extensive learning and acquirements of the lamented author, which would hand down his name to posterity as one of the gifted of the 19th century."—*National Intelligencer.*

"A posthumous work, and a noble monument to the memory of the distinguished Professor, whose loss in the Arctic created such an intense sorrow in the city of his birth, education, and active life, and such an overwhelming sense of calamity wherever his just fame had spread."—*Home Journal.*

"These lectures, or rather essays, are of surpassing beauty and excellence. We know not where to look for a volume so admirably adapted to the wants of a large class of young readers, who desire to direct their reading intelligently and profitably."—*Boston Traveller.*

"This is one of the most thoughtful and earnest course of lectures we have ever met with."—*Boston Transcript.*

"They evince profound knowledge of the springs of English literature. and are imbued with genial sentiment, fine discrimination, and critical acumen."—*N. Orleans Bee.*

"This is a volume written with strength, edited with feeling, and published with taste. * * * The mild and thoughtful countenance of the author, neatly engraven on steel, will be found a valuable memento to his many surviving friends."—*Newark Daily Advertiser.*

"A more creditable book, of the same bulk, has never issued from the American press. And if it does not receive a prompt and hearty welcome in every section of our country, then, we confess, we shall be greatly disappointed. If Talfourd, or Southey, or some other Englishman of celebrity, had produced a work of such genial criticism as this, it would, very justly, have added to his fame. It would speedily be caught up and reprinted here, and thousands of copies would, in a few weeks, be distributed from Maine to Louisiana. And shall the prophet be less regarded by his own countrymen? We trust not. We cannot believe that a book which we feel sure, Irving, and Ticknor, and Dana, and Prescott will consider as worthy to stand on the same shelf with their own best productions, will be coldly neglected by any who profess to venerate those authors."—*U. States Gazette.*

"These Lectures are instructive, eloquent, and even brilliant; they are the productions of a powerful and refined mind, that is keenly appreciative both of the severest logic and of the most subtle beauties of thought. Every reader must admire them, and acknowledge that he has been profited and entertained by their perusal."—*N. York Observer*

Ladies' Historical Library.

Containing the five popular works described below, bound in uniform style. 9 vols. Cloth, extra, ... $9.00

Memoir of the Empress Josephine.

Historical and Secret Memoirs of the Empress Josephine, first wife of Napoleon Bonaparte. By Mad'lle M. A. Le Normand. Translated from the French by Jacob M. Howard, Esq. With Portraits. Two volumes, 12mo. Cloth, gilt, ... $2.00

"It possesses great intrinsic interest. It is a chequered exhibition of the *undress life* of Napoleon. All the glitter and pomp and dust of glory which bewilder the mind is laid; and we behold not the hero, the emperor, the guide and moulder of destiny, but a poor sickly child and creature of circumstance—affrighted by shadows and tortured by straws."—*City Item.*

"This is one of the most interesting works of the day, containing a multiplicity of incidents in the life of Josephine and her renowned husband, which have never before been in print."—*N. O. Times.*

"This is a work of high and commanding interest, and derives great additional value from the fact asserted by the authoress, that the greater portion of it was written by the empress herself. It has a vast amount of information on the subject of Napoleon's career, with copies of original documents not to be found elsewhere, and with copious notes at the end of the work."—*N. O. Com. Bulletin.*

"Affords the reader a clearer insight into the private character of Napoleon than he can obtain through any other source."—*Balt. American.*

"They are agreeably and well written; and it would be strange if it were not so, enjoying as Josephine did, familiar colloquial intercourse with the most distinguished men and minds of the age. The work does not, apparently, suffer by translation."—*Balt. Patriot.*

Memoirs of Marie Antoinette.

Memoirs of the Court of Marie Antoinette, Queen of France. By Madame Campan, First Lady to the Bedchamber of the Queen. From the third London edition. With a Biographical Introduction from the "Heroic Women of the French Revolution," by M. De Lamartine, Member of the Executive Government of France. New edition, with three additional Chapters. With Portraits. Two volumes. Cloth, extra, $2.00

"The book is a noble defence of Marie Antoinette against the many calumnies breathed against her. Moreover, as a picture of manners during the latter years of Louis XV., and the entire reign of his successor, it has no superior; it is at once more decent and more veracious than the 'Life of Dubarry,' and the thousand other garbled memoirs of that period. A large number of notes, explanatory and otherwise, accompany the volume, and add materially to its value. Messrs. Parry & M'Millan have published the book in a style of great elegance, and illustrated it with portraits, on steel, of Marie Antoinette and Madame Elizabeth. It is a book that should find a place on every lady's centre-table."—*Neal's Gazette.*

"Two very interesting volumes, which the reader will not be likely to leave till he has finished them."—*Public Ledger.*

"The material of this history could not have emanated from a more authentic or official source, nor have been honoured with a more distinguished or capable godfather than De Lamartine."—*Saturday Courier.*

"These elegant volumes are a reprint from the third London edition of this very delightful work. The vicissitudes depicted in the volumes, and scarcely less the charming style of the author and the entire familiarity of her theme, make the work one of the most interesting that has recently issued from the American press, and no less instructive and entertaining."—*N. Y. Com. Adv.*

"This delightful work, abounding with historical incidents connected with one of the most stirring periods of French history, presents the reader with the personal annals of one of the most amiable and excellent women that ever shared the honours of royalty."—*Baltimore Sun.*

MEMOIRS OF ANNE BOLEYN.

Memoirs of the Life of Anne Boleyn, Queen of Henry the Eighth. By Miss BENGER, author of "Memoirs of Mrs. Elizabeth Hamilton." Second American, from the third London edition. With a Memoir of the Author, by Miss Aikin. With Portrait. 1 vol. Cloth, . $1.25

"There is no more romantic chronicle in history than the story of Anne Boleyn, as we trace her progress up to the throne and then down to the scaffold. We know no work which gives us a better view of private and domestic life in England in that day, and can confidently recommend it as a delightful piece of biography, valuable for the information it imparts, and narrating adventures which keep up the interest to the end."—*Albany Register.*

"No more valuable or instructive work can be added to a general library."—*Newark Advertiser.*

MEMOIRS OF MARY, QUEEN OF SCOTS.

Memoirs of the Life of Mary, Queen of Scots; with Anecdotes of the Court of Henry II., during her residence in France. By Miss BENGER, author of the "Memoirs of Anne Boleyn." With Portrait. Two volumes, 12mo., ... $2.00

"From very flattering reviews of this work, that have appeared in English publications and a perusal of the eventful life of Anne Boleyn, we had anticipated a very agreeable treat, and our expectations have been more than realized. Miss Benger has a most happy faculty of condensing historical information, and while occupied in portraying the events of Mary's career, gives the reader a bird's-eye glance at those institutions and laws which contributed, while a resident in France, to the formation of her character, and at the same time introduces on the stage the prominent actors, whose influence or example may have had an influence over her. Her description of the Court of Henry II. cannot fail to interest the reader, for she descends at times to details, which possess all the attractions of romance, but which are strictly historical. An objection may be urged to her copious notes, many of which might have been incorporated in the text, without injury, but her desire probably to authenticate every fact of any importance, has been the cause of this, and by the critical reader will be deemed as essential. No lengthy review of this work is necessary to insure it a perusal from our readers, for no reader of history can fail to take a deep interest in the unfortunate Mary; and our friends, who are preparing volumes for winter evening perusal, will find these every way worthy their attention."—*Boston Evening Gazette.*

"In these days of shabby reprints, it is a treat to get hold of a publication in the best style of type and paper, for which Messrs. Parry & M'Millan are famous. We have not, for a long time, seen two such beautifully printed volumes."—*Evening Bulletin.*

MEMOIRS OF THE QUEENS OF FRANCE.

Memoirs of the Queens of France. By Mrs. FORBES BUSH. From the last London edition. With Portraits. 2 vols., 12mo. Cloth, . $2.00

"Mrs. Forbes Bush is a graceful writer, and in the work before us has selected the prominent features in the lives of the Queens with a great deal of judgment and discrimination. These memoirs will be found not only peculiarly interesting, but also instructive, as throwing considerable light upon the manners and customs of past ages."—*Western Continent.*

"We have looked over the lives of some of the Queens, presented in these volumes, with great interest. While none are devoid of some degree of attraction, the most of them have a charm about their person or character exceeding anything we find in the most popular romances. They are full of sentiment and romance, rendered all the more touching from the graceful drapery in which they are adorned, and by the truthfulness of which the reader is strongly impressed. It is of course doubly attractive, in reading the strongly marked characters of history, to feel a conviction of the truth with which even the wildest and most thrilling incidents are invested. The lives of these fair ladies are full of instruction, a merit that mere romance seldom possesses. The author, Mrs. Forbes Bush, commences with Queen Basine, in the reign of Childeric I., or about four hundred years after the commencement of the Christian era. The volumes close with the late Queen of the French, Marie Amelie."—*Saturday Courier.*

SIGOURNEY'S (MRS.) POEMS.

Illustrated Poems. By Mrs. L. H. SIGOURNEY. With designs by F. O. C. Darley, engraved by distinguished artists. With beautiful Portrait of the Author, by Cheney, after Freeman. Handsomely bound in cloth, super extra, ... $5.00
Turkey morocco, extra gilt, ... 7.00

LIST OF ILLUSTRATIONS.—The Divided Burden—A Landscape—Oriska—The Ancient Family Clock—Eve—The Scottish Weaver—The Indian Summer—Erin's Daughter—The Western Emigrant—The Aged Pastor—The Tomb—The Drooping Team—The Beautiful Maid.

"The volume is a most luxurious and gorgeous one, reflecting the highest credit on its 'getters up;' and we know of nothing from the American press which would form a more acceptable gift-book, or a richer ornament for the centre-table. Of the Poems themselves it is needless to speak."—*Y. Blade.*

"In the arts of typography the volume is unsurpassed; the illustrations are numerous and beautiful, and the binder's skill has done its best. Of its contents we will not speak flippantly, nor is it needful that we should say anything. The name of Mrs. Sigourney is familiar in every cottage in America. She has, we think, been more generally read than any poetess in the country, and her pure fame is reverently cherished by all."—*N. O. Picayune.*

"It is illustrated in the most brilliant manner, and is throughout a gem-volume."—*Pa. Inquirer.*

"This work, so beautifully embellished, and elegantly printed, containing the select writings of one of the most celebrated female poets of America, cannot fail to be received with approbation."—*Newburyport Paper.*

"The illustrations are truly beautiful, and are exquisitely engraved. They are from designs by Darley, who has risen to high eminence in his department of art. The entire execution of the volume is a proud evidence of growing superiority in book-making on the part of American publishers. And this liberality has not been displayed upon a work unworthy of it."—*N. Y. Com. Adv.*

SIGOURNEY'S NEW VOLUME OF POEMS.

The Western Home, and other Poems. By Mrs. L. H. SIGOURNEY. In one handsome volume, 12mo. Cloth, ... $1.25
Cloth, extra, ... 1.50

"This volume is an entirely new contribution, which its highly esteemed author makes to the national literature, of which she has so long been a distinguished ornament. The *Western Home*, which constitutes the leading poem of the volume, among other touching incidents, pictures in glowing verse some of the events in the career of Burr, and his unfortunate victim, Blennerhasset, whose history and unhappy fate live among the brightest as well as darkest memories of the mighty West."—*American Courier.*

"Mrs. Sigourney is, perhaps, the most popular of our female poets. The longest poem in this volume is a truthful and beautiful panorama of the early settlement of Ohio, and should be read in every 'Buckeye' family. We commend it to all lovers of good poetry."—*Cincinnati Christian Herald.*

"There are passages of true poesy in the *Western Home*, which for melody, rhyme, force of expression, and regularity of metrical arrangement, are nowhere to be surpassed."—*Boston Gazette.*

"More brilliant poetry, doubtless, can be found in all the popular periodicals of the day; but the genuine household flavor of Mrs. Sigourney's productions, and their natural delineation of universal feelings, will long recommend them to popular favour."—*N. Y. Tribune.*

SIGOURNEY'S SELECT POEMS.

Select Poems, by Mrs. L. H. SIGOURNEY. With illustrations. New edition. In one handsome volume, 12mo. Cloth, ... $1.25
Cloth, extra gilt, ... 1.50

"Mrs. Sigourney has written more than any other female author of this country, and for teaching others of her sex holy and profitable truths, she is unsurpassed."—*Cincinnati Chronicle.*

www.ingramcontent.com/pod-product-compliance
Lightning Source LLC
LaVergne TN
LVHW011213110826
845150LV00006B/1414